Pathway to Glory

Keys to Christian Living

Lila B. Mullins

To: Angie —
May you receive
a special blessing
as you read.

Lila B. Mullins

Psalm 37:4

Pathway to Glory

You guide me with your counsel,
and afterward you will
take me to glory.

—*Psalm 73:24*

The wise shall inherit glory.

—*Proverbs 3:35*

Dedicated
to
my daughter
LYNN MULLINS WILLIAMS
who motivated me to write this book.

Appreciation

My gratitude to GERTRUDE P. DEESE for editing this book and for advice and encouragement which have been invaluable.

Scripture quotations are taken from the New International Version and the King James Version

The drawings on pages 17, 23, 34 ,39, 45, 52, 54, 58, 61, 67, 69, 76, 81, 91, 102, 114, and 126 are by Dill Beaty.

Cover photo and design by Mike Walker, Limbic Graphics, Nashville, Tennessee.

Additional copies may be ordered from your local bookstore or:

Librom Publishing
2809 12th Avenue South
Nashville, TN 37204
1-800-331-5991

TABLE OF CONTENTS

Preface

I have many things on my mind and I want to share them with you. The only way I can do this is through these observations.

As we travel the pathway of life we will encounter many obstacles; we will meet and come face to face with pain and sorrow. We may become discouraged even to the point of despair.

Through it all we can have a fulfilling and rewarding life if we place Christ front and center, and if we allow Him to lead us as we rely on Him to help us in overcoming any barrier.

I have a firm conviction that the *key* to life—this earthly sojourn as well as eternal life—is found in the Holy Word revealed to us by the Holy Spirit.

Let's use this key to open the door that leads us on the pathway to glory.

Lila B. Mullins

Dawn

Once again I have been blessed to see the dawn of another day. I must hurry to open the blinds to see the majestic entrance of the ribbons of colors as they creep across the eastern horizon. The purple bands are always there fading into various shades of blue, and the sky is blushing with a soft pink hue.

I must grasp this moment quickly, for all too soon the bright colors will leave the stage to make room for the soft blue that forms the background for the sun. I have the urge to clasp the colors in my hands, but they elude me and vanish before my eyes.

How many people will see this breath taking scene as God fulfills his promise?

As long as the earth endures, seedtime and harvest, cold and heat, summer and winter, day and night will never cease.
—Genesis 8:22

All too few I fear. Many are still asleep, while others fail to open blinds and draperies. They must hurry to meet the obligations of the day. They miss the early morning view of God's glory.

I hope that you will take the time some morning soon to drink in this fleeting picture of awe-inspiring magnificence. It may be that God in his infinite wisdom has placed this beauty in the early morning sky to bring the calmness and tranquillity that you will need to face the problems and pressures of the day.

...You have set your glory above the heavens.
—Psalm 8:1

Identity Discovery

Have you ever felt that you had not been given credit for something you alone had accomplished? Or do you feel that you have not been recognized for yourself and what you are? Is your only claim to fame being someone's daughter, wife or mother?

I have this problem. Sometimes I feel like a non-identity. I have always been connected to someone else. First, I was Mrs. Robinson's daughter, then Professor Mullins' wife. Next came Lynn's mother, and now I'm Mark, Jeremy and Nathan's grandmother. Not that I don't take great pride in these links, but sometimes I long to be recognized for myself alone. Is this egotistical? Maybe.

I have always been reserved and usually let others do the talking. (Some may dispute this.) I was told as a child that you learn more by listening than by talking. When two or three women insist on talking at the same time, I wish I had ear plugs.

Attention is not what I'm craving. No way do I want to be center stage. I'm not an understudy waiting in the wings hoping the leading lady will faint so that I can flit on stage and have my moment of glory. Only in recent years have I mustered the courage to speak up in groups or put in my "two cents worth" in meetings. The simple task of conducting devotionals in the garden club took on mammoth proportions until I persuaded myself that I needed and wanted to do this. Finally I conquered, and, at the end of two years, I was able to speak without my knees knocking together, my hands shaking, and my voice trembling. Yet there seemed to be something lacking. I really wanted to be known for something uniquely mine.

I have arranged flowers for over forty years, but no one looks at me and acclaims that I am an outstanding flower arranger. My feeble efforts at painting are gathering dust in my garage. Wouldn't it be funny if some day one of these paintings would be discovered and found to be worth $50,000. Not likely.

Clarence thought I was the best cook in the world. This was the psychology he used, or so he thought, to keep from eating out. "Why should we go out," he said, "when we have better food at home." I tried to tell him that I didn't think I was the best cook and didn't want that particular distinction anyway. Many times I thought of putting a sign on the kitchen door "closed until further notice." The Betty

Crocker Blue Ribbon Award for best banana pudding was not the kind of fame I was seeking.

All of my friends know I'm a quilter, and they want to see my latest creation, but so far I haven't been invited to lecture at the National Quilt Show, much less the International Quilt Show. I dabble in poetry and often compose a poem for a particular person on a specific occasion, yet I have not been named Poet Laureate of Tennessee.

Where can I find my elusive identity? What is lasting anyway? The gold watch, proudly accepted at one time, will stop running. The 25-50 year service pin will be forgotten in a drawer. The blue ribbons will be misplaced. The trophy will lose its gloss and gather dust. The thundering applause following a lecture will be silent. The silver tray will become tarnished. The certificate of merit will turn yellow and crumble.

As wonderful as these things are at the time, there is no permanency. I do not intend to detract from honors bestowed, awards received. They have their place and have a value in self-esteem and confidence in accomplishment. But I'm forgetting something. Yes, that's the answer. I'm a pilgrim in an alien land. The fame and recognition on this earth will one day fade into oblivion, but nothing can take the place of my relationship with my Saviour. I'm God's child: A child of the King, of royal heritage. Nothing can be more wonderful than this. If I remain true to Him, I will someday kneel at the throne of the Lord of lords, the King of kings, and there be recognized as His child.

> *I charge you to keep this command without spot or blame until the appearing of our Lord Jesus Christ, which God will bring about in his own time—God, the blessed and only Ruler, the King of Kings and Lord of lords...*
> —I Timothy 6:14-15

So, hold your applause, keep the trophy on the shelf for something else—no accolades, please!

Did I say I have an identity crisis? Absolutely not!

The Music of Silence

Are you on a fast track going nowhere and unable to see the light at the end of the tunnel? Are you on a carousel going around and around never able to get off. Or are you like the falling leaves caught up in a whirlwind of an unending circle?

Are we as a people suffering from malnutrition of the soul? What about nourishment for the mind? Do we read too many books without quality and see too many movies and T.V. shows which can only be designated as trash? Do we listen to music with no more than a jungle beat and lyrics of a degrading nature, and are we just too busy with jobs, careers, and recreation?

Some people feel the need to have the T.V. or radio on constantly both at home and in the car. Even the runners and joggers wear headphones. What a pity! So many don't know themselves: who they are, what they are, and why.

Why are we compelled to be surrounded with noise? It is hard to find a restaurant with soft music. Usually you are greeted at the door by a blast of music like a bolt of lightning. Conversation is almost impossible in this setting. I can't "hear" myself think.

I have gone to homes and before the door was opened, I could hear the T.V., radio, or tape player. Why so loud? It sounded like a war zone. Have mercy on our eardrums! How can people function in this state of chaos, or am I the one out of step? I think not.

I'm not an opponent of T.V. *per se.* Basketball season will find me in front of the tube more than usual, but I try to be selective with programs? Are we afraid of our own thoughts? Do we not consider ourselves good company? Find the T.V. off button—push down. Explore your own mind and you may discover that you enjoy your own thoughts; hidden talents may surface, and things may come to light that will improve your quality of life.

All of us need to get out of the whirlwind and off the carousel. Getting off a moving vehicle is not easy, even slowing down is hard, but maybe it's time for us to take inventory of every facet and phase of our lives and ask the question, "Where are we going?"

It is good that a man should both hope and quietly wait for the salvation of the Lord.

—Lamentations 3:26

In my own life, a long recuperation from a broken hip has provided me with a period of introspection that I may not have had otherwise. At least, I have a little more patience as it takes me longer to do everything. In moments of quiet reflection, I have come to know myself better.

All of us need to shift into second gear periodically, take time out, get off the interstates and travel the backroads. We will see things in a different perspective. "Take time to smell the roses," they say. Let's also take time to listen to the music. Come with me as we try to find the music of life in silence.

> *But the Lord is in his holy temple: let all the earth keep silence before him.*
> —Habakkuk 2:20

The sudden smile of a precious baby can bring to our hearts a soothing lullaby. An unexpected kiss or hug from a child or grandchild while you are reading or sewing can produce strains of a lovely song. A hand placed in ours at a time of sorrow brings a melody of peace and comfort. An exuberant hug of a friend, when we have been recognized for an accomplishment, is like a brass band playing a patriotic march. Not a single word has been spoken, but the music is there nevertheless.

> *He leads me beside the still waters.*
> —Psalm 23:2

> *Be still, and know that I am God.*
> —Psalm 46:10

When have you walked in the woods in autumn and heard the fire song of the brilliant leaves? Later as the leaves fall and the trees are asleep, we hear the music of rest, and as we watch the squirrels hide their acorns, we might hear the song, "He Will Provide."

Walking alone or with a companion at twilight as the sun sets and shadows fall, we might think of the song:

> *Now the day is over, night is drawing night;*
> *Shadows of the evening steal across the sky.*

The stars sing to us as they shine their tiny lights:

> *Walking alone at eve and viewing the skies afar,*
> *Bidding the darkness come to welcome each silver star.*

15

Day is dying in the west; Heav'n is touching earth with rest,
Wait and worship while the night sets her evening lamps alight thro'
all the sky.

The sudden appearance of rainbow lifts our spirits and brings a warm glow reminding us of God's promises as our hearts sing:

Tis true, O yes it's true, God's wonderful promise is true,
For I've trusted and tested and tried it,
And I know God's promise is true.

The early morning is my favorite time of day. Everything is so fresh and unspoiled, almost a new beginning. As the pink and blue morning glories unfold their beauty and the birds give their wake-up call, the music we may hear is:

The little flow'r that opens,
The little bird that sings
God made their glowing colors,
He made their tiny wings.
(From: "All Things Bright and Beautiful")

What comes to mind as you stand in awe of majestic mountains, powerful and overwhelming?

When I look down from lofty mountain grandeur...
Then sings my soul, my Savior God to thee;
How great Thou art, how great Thou art!

Our mediation need not be sitting on the floor in cross-legged position with hands folded, but in quiet reflection looking inward where we discover our true selves found only in His word and in obedience to our Savior, Jesus the Christ.

And that ye study to be quiet, and to do your own business, and to work with your hands...

—I Thessalonians 4:11

...that we may live peaceful and quiet lives in all godliness and holiness.
—I Timothy 2:2

After much soul searching, and perhaps some changes in our lives such as walking with a slower pace, and after listening to the beautiful music of silence, then we can loudly sing,

Joy to the world, the Lord is come
Let earth receive her King!

Bursting Bubbles

Did you blow bubbles when you were a child? I did. It is such a simple thing, but it can bring much pleasure. Did you try to make the bubble bigger and bigger hoping it would not burst? Did you have a bubble pipe? You could blow and run, and the bubbles would trail in the breeze. The colors were so beautiful and transparent.

Life is full of bubbles. Some burst accidentally and others on purpose. We burst our own bubbles, and sometimes we burst the bubbles of other people. We may have burst someone's bubble unintentionally by making a thoughtless remark. At other times we may have burst someone's bubble because of a tinge of jealousy. When a special honor or award has come to a friend, or some happiness has come into their lives, before we realize it, we burst their bubble by saying something negative, a cutting remark, or an unkind quip.

Each day determine that you will control your tongue—think before you speak, and rejoice in another person's good fortune.

The lips of the righteous know what is fitting.

Proverbs 10:32

Reckless words pierce like a sword but the tongue of the wise brings healing.
—Proverbs 12:18

If anyone considers himself religious and yet does not keep a tight rein on his tongue, he deceives himself and his religion is worthless.
—James 1:26

A Thread and a Prayer

All of us have heard the saying, "When life hands you lemons, make lemonade." Have you heard this one, "When life gives you scraps, make quilts"? A friend traveling through Arkansas saw this sign in a craft shop.

What do you do in crises? How do you handle disappointments, failures, illness? How do you cope with shattered dreams, the loss of a loved one, or a broken heart over a love not destined to be? What is the recipe for the lemonade? How can we piece the scraps together to complete a harmonious design that will put our lives back together again?

How are we supposed to react to these various situations as we travel the highway of life with its pitfalls, detours, setbacks, and deadends? What is our attitude and what does God expect of us? Has he given any guidelines are sign posts to aid us in the way we cope?

Usually when people ask us, "How are you?" we say, "Fine." "How are things with you?" we say, "Good." Do we really feel this way, or do we want to dismiss the question, or, maybe, we answer automatically without thinking. Are we reticent and sometimes silent in regard to problems or trials? All of us are different, and no two persons handle the same problem in exactly the same way. Is there a criterion on which we should base our actions?

In my pilgrimage of 75 years I have met many people from all walks of life, different cultures, and backgrounds, but in each there is the same thread that cries, sometimes silently, for help from some source. The silent type may not want to be vulnerable, or does pride enter the picture? There may be a feeling of the stripping away of the veneer in which so many of us cloak ourselves.

On the other hand, we all know someone who, when asked the same question, "How are you?" immediately goes into a lengthy account and gives every detail of the latest trip to the doctor and all the things that may be wrong, some of them imaginary. We knew better than to ask in the first place, but somehow the question slipped out.

There are other types. Those who begin to tell their problems, and you feel that they want to share with you and desire your input and advice; then all of a sudden the curtain is drawn and the door closed. What happened? Is this as far as he or she intended going in the first place, or did they suddenly realize they did not want to bear their soul?

There is still another class who feel the need and desire to share the tragedies that have come into their lives, and they find real relief in the outpouring. It is not that they share with everyone but do feel comfortable in telling a close friend.

There are some women who are revealing now that they are the victims of rape, incest, and/or child sexual abuse. They feel that this revelation frees them, brings peace and release. They feel, too, that this knowledge will help others reveal a similar situation and end it sooner. I don't think everyone can do this or that it is always best, but if a person believes that it is, then it is an individual decision.

What is the best way? What about sin in our lives and in the lives of family members? Do we bring everything out, past and present? Do we really need to tell that old Uncle Joe was a moonshiner, or that a great grandfather had killed a man in anger? What about Cousin Louie riding with Jesse James, and there's prudish Aunt Lucy who once had an illicit love affair about which only a handful of relatives know. Also, the lovely Christian woman now in her 80's or 90's who conceals the fact that in her youth and desperation she had an abortion—a sin long since repented of.

Many people, who in their youth sowed their share of wild oats, are now preachers, teachers, church leaders, faithful children of God. Is it necessary or wise to open Pandora's box, or the cobwebbed closet, and let the ghosts of the past fly out to open old wounds and inflict pain and sorrow?

Confess your faults one to another and pray for one another, that ye may be healed...
—James 5:16

What does this mean? Unless there is a reason that will affect lives in the future, the secrets of the past are best left buried. Confession is for the present. Each day we need to confess our sins, shortcomings, and mistakes to our Heavenly Father, but these need not be shared unless you feel that a friend could help with a particular fault. Patience is so hard to deal with and we might say to a friend, "I'm having a hard time being patient; will you pray for me?" or, "I talk too much; please pray that I can control my tongue."

Public confession enters the picture when a sin is generally known. Then, in order to wipe the slate clean, we must be willing to humble ourselves and repent publicly. At this time we break the thread of the past that fastened us to this dreadful sin, be it alcoholism, infidelity, dishonesty, or forsaking the Lord entirely. At this point, it is time to sweep out the clutter and trash from the dark corner, close the closet door, and throw away the key. Erase as much as possible from this page of memories.

What about illness, death, and disappointments? The only answer is prayer. Freely admit to God that you can't handle it alone and plead for his help.

Hear me when I call, O God of my righteousness...have mercy upon me and hear my prayer.

—Psalm 4:1

He will regard the prayer of the destitute...

—Psalm 102:17

And all things, whatsoever ye ask in prayer, believing, ye shall receive.
—Matthew 21:22

What a blessed thought! What a privilege! No problem is too small to bring before His throne; no problem is too large and over powering. God is always waiting for us, but we must ask for His help. There is no sin too dark or too ugly that we can not lay at His feet. Just as an earthly father wants to help an erring child, God holds out arms of compassion, mercy, and forgiveness.

Pride is an enemy, and until we can break the thread of pride that relentlessly binds us are we able to face reality. Only when we drop the facade can we humbly bow before God and say, "Please help me."

Remember the old song, "Take It To the Lord In Prayer"?

Are we weak and heavy leaden, cumbered with a load of care,
Precious Savior still my refuge, take it to the Lord in prayer.

Another song of comfort is "What a Friend We Have in Jesus."

Do we really avail ourselves of this wonderful gift of pouring out our hearts and souls to the Heavenly Father who waits for us to come to Him? Do we truly believe that He will help with our burdens and problems?

Come unto me all ye that labor and are heavy laden, and I will give you rest. Take my yoke upon you and learn of me; for I am meek and lowly in heart; and ye shall find rest unto your souls. For my yoke is easy, and my burden is light.

—Matthew 11:28-30

Does any good come from adversity, and is there an unseen value in serious illness? Will a special blessing appear to help ease the pain and soften the blow of tragedy?

Therefore I take pleasure in infirmities, in reproaches, in necessities, in persecutions, in distresses for Christ's sake; for when I am weak, then am I strong.

—II Corinthians 12:10

Do we believe this? It's hard sometimes, but our faith convinces us to stand steadfast.

And we know that all things work together for good to them that love God, to them who are called according to his purpose.

—Romans 8:28

Can we find the things that will ultimately work together for good when our lives have been shattered by failures, broken homes, illness, and forsaken by friends and loved ones? Seek and it will surprise you to discover that things are not as bleak as they seem. If you will put yourself in God's hands and allow Him to mold you and reshape you, then the trials can be a time of reflection, spiritual renewal, and maturity. You will view life from a different perspective, and you will be more understanding and compassionate. You will have an insight not available before; you will discover that you have acquired His peace which passes all understanding.

Through trials, tribulations, and adversities we can help others. Only after your darkest night of suffering can you sit by the bedside of another with empathy. Only when *you* have stood by *your* husband's grave can you take the hand of a friend and say, "I understand." Only when you have gone through the valley of shadow of death can you truly appreciate the wonderful gift of life. Only when *you* have experienced the heartbreak of a love gone wrong, or one that was not meant to be, can you dry the tears of the young woman and say, "I know; I've been there." Only when we have survived the rainstorm can we appreciate the rainbow.

21

Break the threads of doubt, fear, uncertainty, and despair, and weave each day through with prayer and thanksgiving. Then that lemonade will have the exact sweetness, and the scraps will result in a quilt of beauty—a constant reminder that:

I can do everything through Him who gives me strength.
—Philippians 4:13

Break the thread that hinders you in service to the Lord; break the thread of indifference; break the thread of hopelessness and insecurity. Lay every burden at His feet; enter the palace of prayer and hold to God's unchanging Hand.

As the Parade Passes By

Everybody loves a parade, from the young child held in arms to the oldest, grey haired person. There is something so exciting and exhilarating about the marching bands, the festive costumes, the clowns, and the beauty queens. Even the animals seem to sense their importance as they prance and strut to the delight of old and young.

There are different kinds of parades. Patriotic parades bring a sense of pride for our country; a respect and honor for those who served our country either in wartime or peacetime; also a remembrance of those who made the supreme sacrifice. There is nothing quite like a military band to stir the emotions.

The Thanksgiving Day parade ushers in the holiday season and provides the mood for shopping, parties and gift giving, and more especially, hopefully, a time for thinking of those less fortunate and providing for them.

What can be more exciting for a child than the Christmas parade when that grand old man, Santa Claus, once again brings laughter and joy to the children and to those of us who are still young in heart.

Let's not forget the Rose Bowl Parade, the culmination of the football season and the beginning of a new year with its resolutions and hopes and dreams for the future. Then there are the beauty queens, the essence of charm and grace, admired and often envied by many teen age girls.

In small towns and rural communities there are parades for almost anything. For one day each year the peach, strawberry, pumpkin, to name only a few, take center stage as the parade passes by. In the unlikely town of Fulton, Tennessee there is a banana festival and parade each year.

Up to this point we have been only observers of these parades. Stop a minute; think! Are not all of us participants in the most important parade of all? Are we not observed, watched and even scrutinized by everyone with whom we come in contact? We are probably not aware most of the time of how we appear to others, how we come across, but our traits and character show through when we least expect it. We are daily parading across the stage of life. Not everyone has a starring role, some do not have a speaking part, some are minor characters but all of us are in the one time parade.

Does this bother you, make you self conscious, apprehensive? Are you aware of the impression you make on others or do you even think about it? The most shy and timid person is observed, though you may think that no one notices you or cares what you do or think. Our influence and example is paraded daily for the world to observe whether we realize it or not.

What preparations can we make and what can we do so that we will be viewed in a positive light as we parade through life? How do you want to be remembered? Maybe, that you were a loving father or mother—this is important. Perhaps you are a good teacher, a great speaker or a scholar; again this is important. Will your grandchildren remember you as a good cook, especially a baker of delicious cookies? And you grandfathers—will your grandchildren say that you always had time for them, pointing out the wonders of nature, going fishing, playing ball?

How do you want friends and acquaintances to remember you? That you were kind and caring, a good listener, and always helpful? Did you put others first, were you busy with good works, aware of the poor? Were you concerned with evangelizing? Was the Great Commission on your mind as you paid bills, took vacations, bought things for yourself, many not really needed? Are you and have you been a good steward of what has been on loan to you by God?

....remember the words of the Lord Jesus, how he said, It is more blessed to give than to receive.

—Acts 20:35

Blessed is he that considers the poor: the Lord will deliver him in time of trouble.

—Psalm 41:1

Give, and it will be given to you. A good measure, pressed down, shaken together and running over, will be poured into your lap. For with the measure you use, it will be measured to you.

—Luke 6:38

What kind of footprints are you leaving on the sands of time as you march daily in the big parade? If you are a Christian and have submitted your life to Him, ask Him to guide you and lead you, then you're on the right track. If you are a prominent speaker, teacher, or writer, fall on your knees every day and thank God for this ability, praying that you will have the proper influence and realizing your responsibility and the impact you have on others.

If you are an artist, do you appreciate this talent you have through the stroke of a brush? You can create scenes of lasting beauty. Thank God for this. And the musician—without music our world would be a drab and dreary place. It brings you, tears, calmness, exhortation, also exhilaration. Praise the Lord if you are a musician.

If you are a good cook, thank God for this talent that brings gladness to others and sustenance to your family. If you are a seamstress or a quilter, thank your Heavenly Father for this talent that enables you to leave behind tangible evidence of your presence in the parade.

But you say that you don't have any of these talents. Wait a minute! You can't get off this easily. We need wise people to make decisions, to be good listeners, encouragers, exhorters. You say you don't have wisdom—why don't you? All you have to do is ask; it is only a prayer away.

Wisdom is the principal thing; therefore get wisdom: and with thy getting, get understanding.

—Proverbs 4:7 (KJV)

If any of you lacks wisdom, he should ask of God, who gives generously to all without finding faults, and it will be given to him. But when he asks, he must believe and not doubt, because he who doubts is like a wave of the sea, blown and tossed by the sea.

—James 1:5, 6 (NIV)

You can surely write a note of encouragement to someone who is sad, sick, or discouraged. This may be the thing most needed at this time. For someone who is very unhappy and blue, you can say, "If you don't have a smile today, I'll give you one of mine."

If you will hold to God's unchanging hand, accept his grace, and abide in his love, you can march confidently in the parade. Remember, though, the parades we view pass all too soon: the clowns are gone before we had time to see them all, and we missed some of the animals as they hurried by. Our lives go by quickly, like a vapor that appears briefly, like a watch in the night. We must seize each moment and every opportunity. Our parade is a one time performance so we must make the most of it.

....what is your life? You are a mist that appears for a little while and then vanishes.

—James 4:14

Hasten! Get on the bandwagon before the parade passes by.

The Corners of Your Mind

Have you ever thought about corners? What is a corner? It is the place where converging sides meet. It is difficult to get out of a corner. Sometimes we say, figuratively, "he/she has me backed into a corner."

In our houses corners collect dust and often are a haven for lost articles. If we don't know where to put something, we say, "Put it in the corner."

What things are in the corners of your mind? Maybe you have placed things there thinking you will deal with them later. A corner can become a place of delayed action. Or have you hidden things in a corner hoping they will remain there and never be brought to light? Is one of your corners collecting dust, stagnant and inactive? Now, let's clean out the negative corners which may contain neglect, regret, self-pity, envy or hatred.

In a more positive light, we should use a corner to store memories, some precious, some poignant, which we bring out and relive periodically. The most important thing to put in a corner of our mind is God's word; but we must not allow it to be inactive to be used only when trouble or sorrow comes, or perhaps a crisis or tragedy. God's word must be a part of our daily life. Only through daily study and application of the Holy Scriptures can we be pleasing to God and productive in His Kingdom.

The heart of the righteous studies to answer.
—Proverbs 15:28

Study (give diligence) to show thyself approved unto God, a workman that needeth not to be ashamed, rightly dividing the word of truth (handling aright the word of truth).
—II Timothy 2:15

27

Beyond the Locked Door

Mystery stories have always held a fascination for me. When I was a teen-ager I read the Nancy Drew mysteries and many other similar books.

In many of these stories there were secret passages, hidden caves and houses with locked doors. Most often these houses were large and dark with an ominous appearance; and as the story began there would be claps of thunder and streaks of lightening which added to the drama and created a foreboding backdrop and also provided an air of suspense.

As the plot unfolded, it was revealed that a room or a section of the house was locked or closed. From this point, the reader was lead, very slowly, by the author to the discovery of what was beyond the locked door.

In *The Secret Garden* there was a room with the door locked and inside was a boy ten years of age, shut away from the outside world because he was ill and frail. He was an embarrassment to his father who thought he was protecting his son, but, actually, he was keeping him from living a normal life.

Many people have locked doors, literally, while some have them locked in their minds. There was a time when no one said the "C" word, or if spoken at all, it was in hushed tones. For some reason there seemed to be a stigma attached to cancer. Fortunately, this attitude no longer exists.

In the past, many people who were crippled or had crippled children felt a sense of shame that was difficult to deal with. I have heard of crippled people who were shut out from the outside world by relatives because of embarrassment. I suppose this attitude comes from a feeling that everyone wants to be physically perfect.

Many years ago children who were born with Down's Syndrome, or similar conditions, were sometimes hidden in the home or institutionalized. Now we know that this group can be treated and taught; also, they can become an important part of their families.

Mental illness is perhaps the most difficult thing to confront. For relatives of the victim, there are guilt feelings and discomposure of mind. The mentally ill have been misunderstood, and for that reason have been locked behind closed doors in homes as well as in institutions.

I have heard of cases, and I have known a few, in which a relative was so sheltered that close friends did not know the person existed. But with so much progress being made in medical research and technology, we are beginning to deal with mental illness in a more positive way.

Most of us don't know what to say to people who are suffering from mental disorders, or to their relatives. Family members may be in denial. Mentally they have locked it away behind a closed door. At this point in time, mental disorders seem to be rampant as never before. This may be due to stress, pressures, demands on our time, and trying to crowd too many things into our lives.

How do we deal with all the many problems that we might want to lock behind a closed door? If you have such a problem, you may need professional assistance; also, you need a trustworthy friend, a spiritual person, who will listen and be supportive.

A friend loves at all times.
—Proverbs 17:17

...there is a friend who sticks closer than a brother.
—Proverbs 18:24

At one time divorce brought a feeling of shame and disgrace, and many people hid behind a locked door. This group needs love and support of a different nature from that of illnesses. It may be that you can be the confidante to a person who is struggling with all the uncertainties of separation and divorce. If so, listen; then pray together and ask for divine help for both of you.

If you are the one facing divorce or abuse, confide in a trusted friend who is able to help. You may need to consult a Christian counselor and join a support group.

I lift up my eyes to the hills—where does my help come from? My help comes from the Lord, the Maker of heaven and earth.
—Psalm 121:1

We wait in hope for the Lord; he is our help and our shield.
—Psalm 33:20

God is our refuge and strength, an ever present help in trouble.
—Psalm 46:1

One other group sometimes closes the door and locks it. A case in point is the couple who have waited anxiously for months in anticipation of the first child. They have decorated the nursery with all the beautiful things so special for a baby; he arrives and they are so happy, but six months later he is taken ill suddenly and dies. The couple is devastated; unable to deal with their grief. They are so overcome that they cannot face the reality, and they close the room leaving everything in place. This is not a healthy way to deal with their grief as they may become withdrawn. Time stands still for them at the time of the death. This couple is in desperate need of someone to help them work through their sorrow. You may be that person.

Let us then approach the throne of grace with confidence, so that we may receive mercy and find grace to help us in our time of need.
—Hebrews 4:16

If you have a locked door in your life, unlock the door and throw away the key.

Alien Alley

When we think of an alley we usually think of a narrow passage between buildings most often at the rear; but did you know that the dictionary in its definition of "alley" lists the number one meaning as "a garden or park walk bordered by trees or bushes"? So let's use the number one meaning as we explore alien alley.

Now what is an alien? We might think of E.T. or some other imaginary being from outer space. The dictionary defines "alien" as a person of another family, race or nation; a person still subject to or a citizen of a foreign country. All of us know what foreign means: situated outside a place or country; situated outside one's own country.

If you have been to a foreign country, you were an alien there. Maybe you didn't think about it unless an incident brought it to mind. When I went to Santo Domingo, Dominican Republic in the 70's, our chartered plane forgot to return for our group. A lack of communication between the tour director and the charter company caused a very inconvenient and uneasy situation.

When we visit a foreign country where little English is spoken, we feel alienated, frustrated and maybe even threatened. But we are forgetting something very important. No matter what country we live in or what language is spoken, we are aliens on this earth traveling down the garden walk surrounded by trees, bushes, and flowers that God has placed here for us to enjoy as we journey through alien alley.

Many of us, far too many, forget that we are aliens in an alien land. We rush here and there, seeking our fortune, looking for pleasure, hoping for fame or power. In our haste for these things we forget that at best we are on earth only a short time.

What is your life? You are a mist that appears for a little while and then vanishes.

—James 4:14

This being the case do we forget about acquiring wealth? No, the wealthy person can contribute so much to others; that is, evangelism, education for those in need, even aiding the hungry and homeless.

Do we forget pleasure altogether? No! The old saying, "All work and no play makes Jack a dull boy" has merit. We need a certain amount of recreation to rejuvenate us so that we can do our work better.

Are fame and power bad things? Not in themselves. It is a question of how they are used. People who have acquired the right kind of fame can be an inspiration to others. People who have right motives and power can get things done.

So how do we balance the scales? God has given each of us certain talents and He expects us to use them in a productive way. He wants us to be happy during our sojourn and has placed us on a garden walk surrounded by the beauties and wonders of nature. We must put everything in its proper perspective. Seek His kingdom first, put Christ at the forefront of your life and the other things will be added.

32

Don't be apprehensive as you walk down alien alley but having confidence that if you have surrendered your life to Him, he will come back some day to take you to your heavenly home that He has prepared for you.

In my Father's house are many mansions; if it were not so, I would have told you. I go to prepare a place for you. And if I go and prepare a place for you, I will come again, and receive you unto myself; that where I am, there ye may be also.

—John 14:2, 3

Prayer

If I have to leave soon now, Lord then take me by your Hand, I know I cannot remain here—this is only an alien land.
I know full well this is not my home, but it is so hard to break away.
My home is with you in another land; I'm ready whenever you say.

The Basket Carriers

Baskets have always fascinated me. They come in different shapes and sizes; some have handles, some don't. They are made of different materials; there are paper baskets, wooden baskets, pottery baskets, but the ones I like are woven. I have always enjoyed watching Indians and other weavers take narrow bands of straw and very meticulously and quickly weave in and out, over and under, and create a beautiful basket.

What do people do with baskets? The basket is very prominent during Easter. It would be unthinkable not to have a basket; that is, if you are a child. It must have a handle in order to carry the eggs.

What about Little Red Riding Hood's basket? In all the illustrations, her basket is pictured as rectangular with rounded corners. It has a wide handle and has a white napkin flowing over the sides.

Then there are market baskets for shopping, mainly replaced by shopping bags, but years ago women carried their own baskets to the grocery. They still do in many countries. In the Caribbean and other areas baskets are carried on the head. It is amazing to see how large, heavy baskets are balanced carefully on the head.

Don't forget the bread basket passed during a meal. It may be quilted, woven, pottery, fine china or even sterling silver. If you have ever lived in the country or visited where chickens are raised, you are familiar with the egg basket. It is carried to the hen house to use in gathering the eggs.

Fruit baskets are popular; sometimes called sunshine baskets. All of us have sent them and have been recipients. They are always a nice surprise.

Baskets are most often used for flowers. What would a wedding be without flowers? Baskets of flowers are a source of comfort and consolation at funerals. For birthdays, anniversaries and receptions, baskets of beautiful flowers make the setting complete.

What do you carry in your basket? You say, "I don't carry a basket." Of course you do. I'm not concerned about the material of your basket, or the shape, or size, but I'm concerned about its contents. Let's find out what you and I carry in our baskets.

Some people carry grudges, unable to get rid of them or unwilling to do something about them. Others carry grief for too long a time, robbing themselves of a productive life. They have stopped in a time frame and a Christian should not do this.

Pride rears its ugly head from many baskets.

When pride comes, then comes shame.

—Proverbs 11:2

Pride goes before destruction, and a haughty spirit before a fall.

—Proverbs 16:18

A man's pride shall bring him low: but honor shall uphold the humble in spirit.

—Proverbs 29:23

Pride can make your basket unusually heavy. Get rid of it!

Sensitivity rides in many baskets. It is an unpleasant thing to have around. Toss it out!

Regret is in many baskets. We cannot undo the past, but we can eliminate regret. Guilt is another item in our baskets that we must not allow to remain. Guilt eats away and destroys us. Throw it out!

Unfortunately, envy is in some baskets. It is so ugly and brings out the worst in people. It can mushroom until it destroys.

A heart at peace gives life to the body, but envy rots the bones.

—Proverbs 14:30

Deceit and hypocrisy rear their heads at times. They will mar and completely ruin lives. Hatred is so terrible that we won't mention it, or shall we? If by chance you are lugging a bit of hatred, don't allow it to stay another minute.

Better a meal of vegetables where there is love, than a fattened calf with hatred.

—Proverbs 15:17

Now what do we put in our baskets? What are the replacements? Let's put love in our baskets first.

Love the Lord your God with all your heart and with all of your soul and with all your strength.

—Deuteronomy 6:5

Do not seek revenge or bear a grudge against one of your people, but love your neighbor as yourself.

—Leviticus 19:18

A friend loves at all times....

—Proverbs 17:17

...Love your enemies and pray for those who persecute you....

—Matthew 5:44

My command is this: Love each other as I have loved you.

—John 15:12

Joy is a beautiful word—put it in next.

These things I remember as I pour out my soul: how I used to go with the multitude, leading the procession to the house of God, with shouts of joy and thanksgiving among the festive throng.

—Psalm 42:4

A basket of songs is a companion of joy. When we sing our hearts are filled with joy, the joy that comes from knowing the Savior and thanking Him for his wondrous love. I dislike saying this, but I see many Christians that do not appear to be joyous. Of all people, Christians should be joyful. We have a Savior, Jesus Christ, who has borne our sins and we are free of this burden. We have His grace and love: He gives courage and strength.

I see many Christians not singing in the worship services. Shame! This is very disturbing to me. By singing praises to our God, we show appreciation for what he has done for us. We sing with joy because we are children of the King.

I will sing unto the Lord...

—Exodus 15:1

Sing to Him, sing praises to Him, tell of all His wondrous acts.

—I Chronicles 16:9

I will sing of Your love and justice; to you, O, Lord, I will sing praise.

—Psalm 101:1

....I will sing with the spirit; and I will sing with the understanding, also.
—I Corinthians 14:15

What a beautiful word peace is. All of us desire peace; peace in the world, peace in the home and peace of mind; so we must put a good measure of peace in our baskets.

....seek peace, and pursue it.
—Psalm 34:14

....Have salt in yourselves, and have peace one with another.
—Mark 9:50

...be of one mind, live in peace; and the God of love and peace shall be with you.
—II Corinthians 13:11

Oh how hard it is to have patience, and yet all of us need more. The attainment of patience takes hard work and self-control but our baskets will be incomplete without it.

A patient man has great understanding but a quick tempered man displays folly.
—Proverbs 14:29

Like a city whose walls are broken down is a man who lacks self-control.
—Proverbs 25:28

A good measure of kindness and goodness must be items in our baskets; and faithfulness, which I like to describe in the simple words of "keeping on, keeping on." We need to be gentle, not harsh and sharp tongued, in our speech and manner of life.

Let love and faithfulness never leave you, bind them around your neck, write them on the tablet of your heart. Then you will win favor and a good name in the sight of God and man.
—Proverbs 3:3, 4

We need one more attribute to make our baskets complete. It is a hard one—self-control. This needs to be worked on constantly for in a flash one can lose control.

Now what do our baskets contain? Fruit, of course.

But the fruit of the spirit is love, joy, peace, patience, kindness, goodness, faithfulness, gentleness and self-control.
—Galatians 5:22, 23

Don't be discouraged if you don't have all of them in the amount you would like. We never reach perfection, but with Christ as our guide we confidently strive for an ample portion of these fruits.

Your basket is not heavy anymore. You have thrown out all of the things that have made your burdens too heavy to bear. Maybe you did not realize that these attitudes were a real hindrance to your Christian life. Now that you have taken inventory and have eliminated the negative and substituted the positive, you can carry your basket with love in your heart and a song of joy on your lips.

Don't you like baskets? I do!

Mending Fences

One of the ugliest sights along our roads and highways is a broken fence. That which was once straight is now crooked; wooden slats lying on the ground beginning to rot. What had been beautiful is now in disarray.

So it is in our lives when our fences become broken, barriers are erected and bridges have collapsed. Life is too short and time is too precious to harbor grudges. Failing to repair damaged relationships eats away at our very being like a terminal illness without hope or cure.

Why are there so many misunderstandings? Some are caused by gossip; the gossip monster takes over at times much like the shadow of King Kong hovering over the Empire State Building. People are too anxious to say, "Have you heard?" "Did you know?" "I can't believe she/he...."

Pride, self-will, and uncompromising attitude and stubbornness are attributes that will prevent us from saying, "Let's clear the air." "We need to talk." "We need to lay our cards on the table." Why is it so hard to say, "I'm sorry, please forgive me if I have done anything to offend you."

Even if you are the one wronged and are waiting for the other person to make the first move, muster the courage and swallow the pride so that you can open the lines of communication. Come down from the platform of pride and admit that the bad feelings are tearing you apart and that you must patch the broken cords in order to have peace of mind.

When pride comes, then comes disgrace, but with humility comes wisdom.
—Proverbs 11:2

Pride goes before destruction, a haughty spirit before a fall.
—Proverbs 16:18

We erect barriers when we fail to admit mistakes or fail to keep the lines of communication open. Pride is a bitter pill but *after* it goes down, sweetness will follow. When you break the ice and say, "We must make things right," a great weight will be lifted from your heart and you can breathe freely again. The ugly shadow that kept you apart from a friend will fade into the warmth of light and love.

Many of us may be too sensitive and wear our feelings on our sleeves. This trait is indicative of a selfish nature. Do we feel that humbleness is a weakness? Not so. Humility is a badge of honor and a strong magnet that draws us back to the course of positive and right thinking.

The fear of the Lord is the instruction of wisdom; and before honor is humility.
—Proverbs 15:33

...all of you, clothe yourselves with humility toward one another, because God opposes the proud but gives grace to the humble.
—I Peter 5:5

Some of the saddest phrases that can be uttered are, "I wish I had said, 'I'm sorry.'" "I wish I had said, 'We need to talk.'" "I wish things had been different." "I wish I had had the courage, now it's too late."

Is there anything in your life that needs correcting, patching up, setting the record straight? Is anything driving a wedge between you and a friend or an acquaintance; or perhaps a relative? If so, please hasten this very day to start the ball rolling or whatever it takes to mend the fences, remove the barriers, and restore the bridges.

Then you can have a clear conscience; you can rest easy; a burden has been lifted. Your heart will no longer be heavy and you will be surprised how happy and wonderful you feel. You will also have the assurance that God is pleased that one more broken fence has been mended.

The Mountain of Mourning

I believe that everyone likes mountains, don't you? Mountains mean different things to different people. For climbers they hold a real challenge, a sense of accomplishment. Some people are interested in the view when they reach the top. For the early settlers the mountains were dangerous obstacles that stood in the way of their efforts to discover new land.

The splendor of mountains has been expressed in songs: "For purple mountain majesties" from "America, the Beautiful"; and who could forget the words from "The Sound of Music": "Climb every mountain, ford every stream."

Mountains have been prominent since the beginning of time. Moses went up into the mountain to receive the Ten Commandments from God (Exodus 31:18).

The transfiguration of Christ took place on a mountain.

After six days Jesus took with him Peter, James and John the brother of James, and led them up to a high mountain by themselves. There he was transfigured before them."

—Matthew 17:2

Christ went to the Mount of Olives to pray before his crucifixion.

And he came out, and went, as his custom was, unto the Mount of Olives; and the disciples also followed him.
And when he was at the place, he said unto them, Pray that ye enter not into temptation.
And he parted from them about a stone's cast; and he kneeled down and prayed.

—Luke 22:39, 40, 41

Most of us will never scale the high mountains of the world. Some people may not be able to stand on the summit of any mountain to view the beauty. Few of us will enjoy mountain hideaways for relaxation, but there is a mountain that each of us, sooner or later, will have to climb; this is the mountain of mourning. There is no escape, no reprieve, no by-pass and no detour.

We would do well to prepare ourselves before we are forced to start the climb. Of course, we cannot completely prepare for the unknown, but we can make the load and burden easier if we study the scriptures that deal with death and mourning.

The first thing we need to do is to face reality. It is so difficult for us to acknowledge that we are pilgrims on a journey, temporarily residing in a pilgrim land. It is so easy to forget; after all, this is the only world we have even known.

Our reminder is recorded in John 14 as Christ comforts his disciples.

> *Let not your heart be troubled; ye believe in God, believe also in me.*
> *In my Father's house are many mansions; if it were not so, I would have told you. I go to prepare a place for you.*
> *And if I go and prepare a place for you, I will come again, and receive you unto myself; that where I am, there ye may be also."*
>
> —John 14:1-3

This is probably the most comforting scripture in the entire Bible, whether we are reflecting on our own mortality or mourning the loss of a loved one.

A passage of scripture that we may not read often is:

> *It is better to go to a house of mourning, than to go to a house of feasting; for death is the destiny of every man; the living should take this to heart."*
>
> —Ecclesiastes 7:2

Jesus, our Savior, knows the struggles we have with mortality and he is compassionate. For this reason he sent the Comforter, the Holy Spirit.

> *And I will pray the Father, and he shall give you another Comforter, that he may abide with you forever.*
>
> —John 14:16

At this point we know that God cares. Also, we know that Christ has sent the Comforter; and that Christ is preparing a home in heaven for us—a home so wonderful and so beautiful that there are not human words to describe it.

God has done his part so now we must do our part in the mourning process. What kind of attitude does God want us to have? We cannot be resentful, bitter or even angry. We cannot say, "God has forsaken me; why did he let this happen?"

God in his infinite wisdom has placed us on earth for a short time, but at the same time, he planned salvation for us through Christ, our Savior, so that we can live forever in a better place.

As you begin the climb, you ask God to help you. You must submit to Him and say, "Thy will be done." Tell Him that you cannot go alone, that you need His strength to lean on and that you must hold to His unchanging hand.

Remember the old song: "Ask the Savior to help you, comfort, strengthen and keep you. He is willing to aid you. He'll carry you through."

Now it is time to enter the grieving period. You cannot ignore what has happened. Separation by death of a loved one is heart rending; we are sad and distraught. This is a time of cleansing, and healing, and retrospection. The time spent at the top of the mountain will vary with different people. Don't stay too long! Don't allow yourself to become withdrawn and reclusive.

Come down now, pick up the pieces and get on with your life. Even though things will never be the same, it is time to make adjustments, make new plans, get involved in activities that help others. This is what God wants you to do.

They will enter Zion with singing; everlasting joy will crown their heads. Gladness and joy will overtake them, and sorrow and sighing will flee away.
—Isaiah 35:10

Near the close of the Bible we have these beautiful and comforting words to sustain and encourage us.

He will wipe every tear from their eyes. There will be no more death or mourning, or crying, or pain, for the old order of things has passed away.
—Revelation 21:4

What consolation! What blessed assurance!

If you have to walk the trail of tears,
If you have to climb the mountain of mourning,
If you sink to the depth of despair—
Remember
Enter the palace of prayer
To receive the calm of the Comforter,
And the peace of our precious Savior.

—Lila B. Mullins

As Autumn Fades

The curtain is slowly closing on another autumn. The leaves have put on their usual show, displaying the various hues and tints of yellow, red, orange and brown. Now, the trees are bare, ready for their rest and winter's slumber. The bare branches are a silhouette against the sky in thinly etched patterns previously concealed by green leaves.

It is early morning—the sky is aglow with colors of beauty impossible to describe by a mere mortal. I see a band of purple that fades into pink with a yellow hue; another band of blue mingled with purple.

O, artist, where is your brush and easel? No, forget it. It would be useless. The master Painter is at work.

When I consider your heavens, the work of your fingers, the moon and the stars which you have set in place...

—Psalm 8:3

Unsung Melodies

Can you imagine the world without music? I can't. Without singing and beautiful melodies, the world would be a dreary place.

There is a saying, "Music soothes the savage beast." Music brings calm and tranquillity into our lives; it revives us when we are tired; it lifts our spirits when we are sad.

Isn't it wonderful that God created us to sing as well as to speak? He could have eliminated our ability to sing, but God knew the joy that singing would give us. Also, God gave us the power to sing because he wanted us to sing praises to Him.

Everyone likes to hear the birds sing. Isn't it amazing that God decided to create the ability to sing to one of the smaller creature in nature? It is so delightful when winter draws its curtain that the birds appear to herald spring with their songs of happiness.

The flowers appear on the earth; the time of the singing of birds is come, and the voice of the turtledove is heard in our land.

—Song of Solomon 2:12

Did you know that Solomon wrote the lyrics to over a thousand songs?

He spoke three thousand proverbs and his songs numbered a thousand and five.

—I Kings 4:32

From the Psalms we learn that David was a great musician and enjoyed singing. Music played a very prominent part in his life.

...my tongue shall sing aloud of thy righteousness.

—Psalm 51:14

I will sing of your love and justice; to you, O Lord, I will sing praise.
—Psalm 101:1

Sing to the Lord a new song, his praise in the assembly of the saints.
—Psalm 149:1

It is very inspiring to read about Paul and Silas as they sang in prison.

About midnight Paul and Silas were praying and singing hymns to God, and the other prisoners were listening to them.
—Acts 16:25

I imagine the other prisoners were astounded, don't you?

Most importantly, is the fact that we are commanded to sing; it is an integral part of our worship and we cannot be pleasing to God unless we participate in praising Him by singing.

Speak to one another with psalms, hymns, and spiritual songs. Sing and make music in your heart to the Lord, always giving thanks to God the Father in everything, in the name of our Lord Jesus Christ.
—Ephesians 5:19, 20

...I will sing with the spirit, and I will sing with understanding also.
—I Corinthians 14:15

I have made an observation which is very disturbing to me—many people do not sing in the worship services; and some who do sing, fail to demonstrate enthusiasm and the proper spirit. This should not be!

I will declare your name to my brothers; in the presence of the congregation I will sing your praises.
—Hebrews 2:12

It may be that some people are afraid of being too emotional. I don't understand this as the word *emotion* means strong feeling, and unless we have exuberance in our singing and praising, we have missed the mark and have not completed our part in the worship services.

The largest group of those not singing are the young people, and this is all the more a matter of great concern. Have they not been taught properly, or do they observe older people not singing? How can we provide the motivation that will encourage them to sing and enjoy praising God?

People who do not sing during the worship services are cheating themselves; and one must put something in the worship in order to get something in return. Remember! You are a participant not an observer; and you must do your part in order to be pleasing to God.

Some people make the excuse that they can't carry a tune and they are embarrassed to sing. God does not require that you have a trained voice or even a naturally beautiful voice. He wants you to express your love and thanksgiving for His blessings in heartfelt hymns of praise.

If you enjoy singing in the worship services and are receiving the blessings that accompany the fruit of your lips, bless you!

...Is anyone happy? Let him sing songs of praise.

—James 5:13

If you are not singing during the worship services, or not as enthusiastically as you should, resolve now to change course and lift your voice in song. I promise that your spirits will be lifted and you will have the satisfaction that you have participated, not merely observed.

"Let Every Heart Rejoice and Sing; Let Choral Anthems Rise."
Don't be a part of the unsung melodies!

And they sing the song of Moses the servant of God, and the song of the Lamb, saying, "Great and marvelous are thy works, Lord God Almighty; just and true are thy ways, thou King of saints."

—Revelation 15:3 (song of the victors who have overcome)

Following the Followers

Did you play follow the leader when you were a child? You were supposed to do everything the leader did; otherwise you were out of the game.

It is necessary to have leaders in everything. Without leaders there is chaos; there is no direction and nothing could be accomplished.

Down through history there have always been causes and movements of various natures, and there always has been a dominant leader. Some people follow a leader because of loyalty; some follow not really knowing much about the matter while others follow in order to be a part of the action.

When Hitler rose to power in Germany, his followers were fanatical in their efforts to please him, even resorting to unspeakable atrocities and murder.

In the business world, when there are unethical or dishonest practices, there will be some employees who will participate for fear of losing their jobs. In the case of a chain of command, climbing the corporate ladder, so to speak, everyone is following the follower above him. Sometimes, good people have been caught up in activities that are questionable, even fraudulent, in fear of losing their position, power and prestige.

Those anxious to climb the social ladder may be willing to overlook dubious standards of conduct in order to be accepted; thus they are following an unworthy leader.

What about youth gangs? These leaders exert an extreme degree of power, influence, and control over their followers because the gangs make them feel that they are a part of something. These people are willing to participate in illegal activities; even murder.

Be not deceived: Evil companionships corrupt good morals.
—I Corinthians 15:33

Whom are we following in our religious lives? You may feel indignation by this question. You say, "I'm following Christ. I'm under his authority. I'm following him." I hope this is true.

It is imperative to have leadership in the church and God has decreed that we have elders; also, he has determined that through preaching we would hear the good news of salvation through Christ.

How then shall they call on him in whom they have not believed? and how shall they believe in him whom they have not heard and how shall they hear without a preacher? and how shall they preach, except they be sent? even as it is written, How beautiful are the feet of them that bring glad tidings of good things!

—Romans 10:14

During the period of the middle and late 1800's and into the early 1900's as the restoration was born, there were differences of opinion. Even though the slogan was, "We speak where the Bible speaks, and are silent where the Bible is silent," it was difficult for everyone to interpret this in the same way.

At that time there were many outstanding leaders and preachers; but some people adhered to one man's belief while others followed the position of another prominent preacher/teacher. Again, it is evident that there were people following the followers.

Traditions played a part in the efforts to return to Biblical authority, but we must take note that tradition is not worth anything unless it is a principle which must be obeyed. We want to be certain that the traditions we are holding to are matters of principle rather than matters of opinion.

It is human nature to be drawn to certain leaders. Some are attractive and some are excellent speakers. Others may have good personalities, and those who are caring and have the ability to assist with problems have a great impact on people.

We want to respect, support, and give heed to our preachers and teachers. Jesus was a preacher.

From that time on Jesus began to preach, "Repent, for the kingdom of heaven is near."

—Matthew 4:17

It was God's plan to convey the gospel through preaching.

He told them, "This is what is written: the Christ will suffer and rise from the dead on the third day, and repentance and forgiveness of sings will be preached in his name to all nations, beginning at Jerusalem..."
—Luke 24:46, 47

I give you this charge: Preach the Word; be prepared in season and out of season; correct, rebuke and encourage with great patience and careful instruction, for the time will come when men will not put up with sound doctrine. Instead, to suit their own desires, they will gather around them a great

number of teachers to say what their itching ears want to hear. They will turn their eyes away from the truth and turn aside to myths.
—2 Timothy 4:2, 3, 4

In addition to listening to our preachers/teachers, every individual Christian has the responsibility of reading and studying the Bible for himself/herself. At times we may be a little lazy as it is easier to sit back and let someone else tell us what the Bible teaches on every subject. We must be active; not passive. We may discover that we are holding to either a tradition or a concept that is not Biblical. We must not be afraid of an open mind and to change.

Don't be afraid of the open Bible! From a diligent study of God's word, you can be assured that you are following the right leader: the Lord, Jesus Christ.

Back to the Back Roads

The interstate highways are amazing, aren't they? That is, if you are old enough to remember when they did not exist. I have always lived in town, but when I was a teenager I visited my uncle who lived on a farm located on a dirt road. During a rainy spell roads would develop ruts and puddles, and mud would splash all over the car, but in dry weather it was a different story. The dust was terrible. When a car passed another car the one behind was victim to a cloud of thick dust. When we traveled, particularly on Sunday morning going to church, we hoped no one would pass us because we didn't want to arrive dirty and dusty, but sometimes this was the case.

The first time I saw architectural drawings of the proposed interstates showing the clover-leafs, I thought they would never work because I thought that the traffic would become snarled ending in a maze. Little did I know.

Now the interstates are an integral part of our world. The 18 wheelers as well as the smallest cars whiz by and appear as a blur. Everyone is in a hurry to meet deadlines, or something; however, some people traveling for pleasure and having the time have decided to take the back roads, the roads less traveled. They are more beautiful, less monotonous, and people can stop when and wherever they like.

What about the highway of life? Are you traveling the interstates, the back roads or the dirt roads? Does it make a difference?

Figuratively speaking, the interstates are filled with the people in a hurry to gain material possessions, prestige, power, and pleasure. They have allowed these things to take hold of their lives and to crowd out spiritual matters. They didn't intend for this to happen but have been caught up in the whirlwind and hurled on to the interstate almost without realizing it.

What about the dry, dusty roads and the wet muddy roads? There is nothing on these roads but stagnation, indecision and lack of ambition—just rocking along eating the dust of the passing cars. This is the unproductive road so we must avoid it.

Let's try the back roads. We can go slowly and strive for balance in our lives. We can make an effort to put everything in proper perspective. Of course, God expects us to provide for our families, educate our children, and have the proper amount of rest and recreation. In order to glorify God and be pleasing to Him, we must be productive, ready for service to others, and all good works.

The people on the interstates and dirt roads have failed to find direction and leadership for their lives. There has to be a captain of the ship, a leader of the pack, a pilot of the plane.

We used to sing a song, "Let Jesus Come Into Your Heart." I have not heard it in a long time, but if we will let Jesus come into our hearts and lives, then we will accept him as our guide and captain.

Jesus said, I am the way, the truth and the life.

—John 14:6

And behold, God himself is with us for our captain.

—II Chronicles

For it became him, for whom all things, and by whom are all things, in bringing many sons unto glory, to make the captain of their salvation perfect through suffering

—Hebrews 2:10

If you are on the interstate, take the next exit and get on the back road; if you are on the dirt road, look for the next sign leading you to the road that will be more positive and productive, and let Christ be your captain.

The back roads are beautiful!

Set up road signs; put up guideposts. Take note of the highway, the road that you take.

—Jeremiah 31:21

The Well of Living Water

I don't know much about wells. I have never drawn water from a well, but when I was a very young child I watched as my uncle drew water from a well.

Wells were very important in Bible times. Everything depended on a good location and whether water would be found after digging. There is no life without water. There is no hope without living water. Where can we find living water?

God chose water as a part of our obedience to His word. Water is a symbol of a burial as we are submerged beneath the water to begin a new life in Him.

In the conversation that Jesus had with Nicodemus, Jesus answered, "I tell you the truth, no one can enter the kingdom of God unless he is born of water and the Spirit" (John 3:5).

When Jesus met the Samaritan woman by the well, he said to her, "If you knew the gift of God and who it is that asks you for a drink, you would have asked him and he would have given you living water (John 4:10).

For the lamb at the center of the throne will be their shepherd; he will lead them to springs of living water. And God will wipe away every tear from their eyes.

—Revelation 7:17

I am Alpha and Omega, the beginning and the end. I will give unto him that is athirst of the fountain of the water of life freely.
                                                    —Revelation 21:6

When we completely surrender our lives to Christ, when we allow Him to guide us, when we love Him and obey Him, then we will have the well of living water. What could be more wonderful! What could be more comforting!

Did you realize that the last paragraph of the Bible reminds us of the source of living water?

...Come! Whoever is thirsty, let him come; and whoever wishes, let him take the free gift of the water of life.
                                                    —Revelation 22:17

Come! Quench your thirst from the well of living water.

A Wall Too Tall—The Load Too Heavy

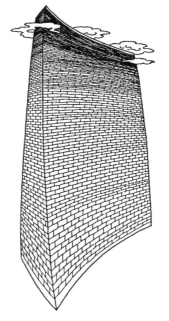

Walls can be many things. For instance, they can be barriers, walls to close off space and divide rooms, and they can function to prevent access to or from some place.

The most prominent wall in the world is the Great Wall of China being the longest structure ever built. Did you know that its length is almost 4,000 miles and that construction was started around 400 B.C.?

The Great Wall was built by China for protection against invaders, but it did not provide defense against Genghis Khan who conquered a large part of China in the 1200's.

In Bible times walls were built around cities for defense, sometimes to keep people in and sometimes to keep people out. What child does not remember the exciting story of Joshua and the battle of Jericho? They sing about the walls tumbling down, and they like to pretend that they are marching around the walls.

> *When the trumpet sounded, the people shouted, and at the sound of the trumpet, when the people gave a loud shout, the wall collapsed; so every man charged straight in, and they took the city.*
> —Joshua 6:20

In this case God planned the strategy for the fall of Jericho, and Joshua and the people followed God's instructions.

The most well known wall in our time was the Berlin Wall that divided East and West Berlin keeping families, friends and lovers apart. Fortunately, this wall has been torn down, and all of us watched on television as it was removed piece by piece.

Life is like a wall: we have obstacles, barriers and burdens: all along the way. Our burdens weight us down and prevent us from making the climb. How can we scale the wall of life when we feel it is too tall and insurmountable? How can we penetrate the barrier when we feel that our burdens are too heavy to carry?

We cannot scale the wall alone; we need help with our burdens. How can the loads be lightened and what is the source of help?

> *Come to me, all you who are weary and burdened, and I will give you rest. Take my yoke upon you, and learn from me, for I am gentle and humble in heart, and you will find rest for your souls. For my yoke is easy and my burden is light.*
> —Matthew 11:28, 29, 30

Some people feel very self-sufficient and they don't want to acknowledge that they need anyone, not even God. Only when they submit to Him and call for help will they be able to rid themselves of the baggage that is too heavy to permit them to climb the wall of life.

> *Even to your old age and gray hairs I am He, I am He who will sustain you. I have made you and I will carry you, I will sustain you and rescue you.*
> —Isaiah 46:4

Don't let pride hinder you; be willing to accept God's help. Let Christ take your burdens and enter into a partnership with Him. Do your part and He will do the part that you are unable to do; then the wall will not be too tall to scale to glorious heights and your load will not be too heavy for you to bear.

Blow the Trumpet in Zion

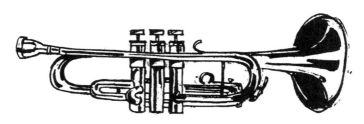

Have you ever thought about the meaning of "Zion"? Many of our hymns refer to Zion, but, as we sing, what is our concept of this word?

We know that Zion was one of the hills of Jerusalem. The temple area was called Zion, and sometimes the whole of Jerusalem. Heaven is called Zion.

> *But you have come to Mount Zion, to the heavenly Jerusalem, the city of the living God.*
>
> —Hebrews 12:22

> *Then I looked, and there before me was the Lamb, standing on Mount Zion, and with him 144,000 who had his name and his Father's name written on their foreheads.*
>
> —Revelation 14:1

> *The Lord dwells in Zion!*
>
> —Joel 3:21

Now, let's talk about trumpets. It is interesting to know that trumpets go back to the time of Moses. The first mention is made in Exodus 19:16, 19. A trumpet was blown to call the people to the assembly. It was also blown to call off pursuit in battle.

Trumpets were blown by watchmen to warn the people of approaching enemies (Ezekiel 33:3). When Solomon was anointed king and also on feast days, trumpets were blown (Psalm 81:3).

> *Blow the trumpet and shout, "Long live King Solomon."*
>
> —I Kings 1:34

The year of Jubilee, celebrated every fifty years, was announced by a trumpet.

Then have the trumpet sounded everywhere.
                                                                —Leviticus 25:9

What child does not know the exciting story of Gideon in the battle against the Midianites? The Lord told Gideon to give trumpets and empty jars to the 300 men, and when the signal was given, they blew their trumpets and broke the jars causing the Midianites to flee in fear (Judges 7).

Why are we talking about Zion and trumpets? What relevance do they have for us in this period of time? I believe we should put on the brakes, slow down, and ponder the brevity of life. We do not know how much time we have even though we may not like to think about it. I fear we are so busy with our daily lives, buying and selling, marrying and giving in marriage, going here and going there. All too soon the shades of night will fall, the last chapter will be written, and the last page will be turned. Our book of earthly life will be closed.

For this reason we need to make more preparation for the other life. We must study the Holy Word more and apply it in our lives in service to others and in evangelism. There are hungry people to feed, physically as well as spiritually. The sick need to be comforted and those who mourn need to be cheered.

We should learn to be selfless instead of self-centered, always remembering the supreme sacrifice that Christ made for us. We should offer a helping hand instead of an empty hand. We will be held accountable for how we have used our words, our time, our talents, and our money. We must be good stewards of the things which have been left temporarily in our care.

When the last song has been sung, the last words spoken, and the last deeds done, we don't want to have regret and remorse.

Life is fleeting! Hurry while it is still day for the night is coming when no man can work, and time shall be no more.

Blow the trumpet in Zion; sound the alarm on my holy hill. Let all who live in the land tremble, for the day of the Lord is coming.
                                                                —Joel 2:1

In a flash, in the twinkling of an eye, at the last trumpet. For the trumpet will sound, the dead will be raised imperishable, and we will be changed.
                                                                —I Corinthians 15:52

Now, brothers, about times and dates we do not need to write to you, for you know very well that they day of the Lord will come like a thief in the night.
—I Thessalonians 5:2

Be ready when the trumpet is blown in Zion!

But I tell you that men will have to give account on the day of judgment for every careless word they have spoken. For by your words you will be acquitted, and by your words you will be condemned.
—Matthew 12:36, 37

Don't Miss the Boat!

Have you ever missed a train, bus, plane or boat? I missed a plane one time through no fault of my own, but, nevertheless, it was still disconcerting.

We "miss the boat" for various reasons. We miss opportunities, we fall short of goals, and we don't carry through to the conclusion. We miss the mark. Why? What are the obstacles that get in the way?

At the beginning of a new year many resolutions are made, but most of them fall by the wayside in a few short months. We miss opportunities sometimes because we are timid or perhaps afraid of failure. We may feel inadequate and don't want to take chances.

We fall short of goals if we set too many or we may not be viewing our situation realistically. We start with enthusiasm, but too many distractions arise, we have to detour, take a side road, and then we are never able to get back on track and we give up.

Another enemy is procrastination; it is the thief of time. We say, "Tomorrow," but tomorrow never comes. Many chances for golden opportunities have been lost because of failure to act at the proper time. Seize the moment!

I believe we will have a better chance of not "missing the boat" if we will slow down rather than be in a hurry. The old adage "haste makes waste" is still true. First, make sure the goals are worthy, seek opportunities; sometimes we have to make our own. We can. We need to have the determination and the will to see things to the end. Don't say, "I can't." Remember the Little Engine that kept saying, "I think I can, I think I can," and he did.

Don't complain and cry about what another person has done or accomplished. Don't look back to what might have been. Be certain that Christ is the center of your life, then you will be able to make better choices. Talk to God in prayer and ask for His help in your decisions. He wants to help you. It will surprise you how much better you will feel and solutions will emerge that were not visible previously.

> *But one thing I do: forgetting what is behind and straining toward what is ahead, I press on toward the goal to win the prize for which God has called me heavenward in Christ Jesus.*
>
> —Philippians 3:14
>
> *I can do everything through Him who gives me strength.*
>
> —Philippians 4:13

Praise and Glory Shortage

Those of you old enough to remember World War II know about shortages. Every commodity you can think of was in short supply and rationing was necessary.

Several years ago there was a shortage of gasoline in this country due to an oil embargo; but we, in the United States, are very fortunate for this is a land of plenty. This is not the case in other parts of the world and is vividly brought to mind daily as we watch and read the news.

Is there a shortage in our spiritual lives? I'm thinking about praise and glory at this time. It seems to me that we don't emphasize praise and glory enough in song or in worship. There are so many passages of Scripture in this regard that it is impossible to list them all here.

Shout with joy to God, all the earth! Sing the glory of his name; make his praise glorious.
—Psalm 66:1, 2

May the peoples praise you, O God; may all the people praise you.
—Psalm 67:3

Enter his gates with thanksgiving and his courts with praise; give thanks to him and praise his name.
—Psalm 100:4

I will exalt you, my God the King; I will praise your name forever and ever. Every day I will praise you and extol your name forever and ever.
—Psalm 145:1, 2

We should praise and glorify our God and our Savior at every service of the Lord's church, and, in addition, we should praise and glorify him daily in our Christian walk. Why? Because:

For ye were bought with a price: glorify God therefore in your body.
—I Corinthians 6:20

I will declare your name to my brothers; in the presence of the congregation I will sing your praise. And again, I will put my trust in him.
—Hebrews 2:12, 13

Our praise should be inspiring and with all the zeal and fervor possible. God is not pleased with half-hearted worship. We should be happy in our worship, not somber. We can still be reverent and at the same time be joyous.

> *Let them praise the name of the Lord, for his name alone is exalted; his splendor is above the earth and the heavens.*
> *Praise him for his mighty acts: praise him according to his excellent greatness.*
> *Let everything that has breath praise the Lord.*

—From Psalm 148

Don't let there be a shortage of deeply felt praise and glory in your life!

> *He who appoints the sun to shine by day, who decrees the moon and stars to shine by night, who stirs up the sea so that its waves roar—The Lord Almighty is his name.*

—Jeremiah 31:35-36

The Balm of Gilead

Often we sing the beautiful song, "There Is a Balm in Gilead." What does it mean? What are our thoughts when we sing it?

Gilead was the mountainous region lying east of Jordan, sometimes called Mount Gilead, sometimes land of Gilead. Balm was a product of Gilead and an article of commerce. It was a fragrant healing ointment that refreshed and soothed, but its exact nature and appearance are unknown. I imagine that many people of that time traveled to Gilead to obtain the balm that would bring relief and comfort from various ailments.

In the spiritual realm what and where is the balm of Gilead? Everybody is looking for happiness and everything that might contribute to the so called "good life." They may be looking in the wrong places. Many people think that material possessions will bring happiness. Others feel that if they had a certain position, several cars, two or three homes, that these things would provide them with happiness. Then there are the workaholics who have become obsessed with their work or projects, or completely absorbed and engrossed to the point that all other facets of their lives have been blocked out. This group is in great need of the balm of Gilead.

Back to the question. Where can we find the balm of Gilead, and how can we have calm, tranquillity, and peace in our lives? How can we be free of pressure, disturbance, and turmoil?

We must ask God for help in finding the balm of Gilead.

Ask and it will be given to you; seek and you will find; knock and the door will be opened to you.
—Matthew 7:7

Many people feel that they don't need anybody; that they have the ability and power to make decisions and choices without God's help. Pride and self-will must be abolished. A do-it-yourself kit is not the answer. We must let God guide us.

I am the way and the truth and the life.
—John 14:6 (Jesus speaking to Thomas)

65

> *Therefore, since we have been justified through faith, we have peace with God through our Lord Jesus Christ, through whom we have gained access by faith into this grace in which we now stand.*
>
> —Romans 5:1

Let go of those things that have held you captive. Throw out the unacceptable, the inadvisable, and the unanchored. Instead hold to an unshakable faith.

> *Rejoice in the Lord always. I will say it again: rejoice! Let your gentleness be evident to all. The Lord is near. Do not be anxious about anything, but in everything, by prayer and petition, with thanksgiving, present your requests to God. And the peace of God, which transcends all understanding, will guard your hearts and your minds in Christ Jesus.*
>
> —Philippians 4:4-7

A life of complete submission to Christ—asking, trusting, and believing—will provide the soothing oil that brings calm and tranquillity. We can sing, "There is a balm in Gilead to make the wounded whole; There is a balm in Gilead to heal the sinsick soul."

If you have accepted Christ as your Savior you have received his grace and the Holy Spirit lives in your heart to comfort you.

> *Peace I leave with you; my peace I give you. I do not give to you as the world gives. Do not let your hearts be troubled and do not be afraid.*
>
> —John 14:27

> *The Lord bless you and keep you; the Lord make his face shine upon you and be gracious to you; the Lord turn his face toward you and give you peace.*
>
> —Numbers 6:24-26

Treasures of the Snow

Each morning as I open the blinds I wonder what will greet me. Although I get the weather report before retiring, the forecast isn't always reliable.

The weather bureau was right this time. An icy fairy land welcomed the new day, as well as a softly falling snow. Silently, the landscape had been clothed in shimmering icicles and every tree branch was bending under the weight of the snow. Everything was wearing a costume of white as though in unison nature had decided to display a breath-taking scene of magnificence.

People react differently to snow. For children it means no school and the opportunity to go sledding, to make a snowman, and to throw snowballs. The eyes of young children light up and dance merrily at the sight of snow.

For people who have to go to work the snow is an inconvenience as well as a danger. Wrecks are numerous because of ice covered highways; traffic moves more slowly or not at all.

Older people have a different view of the snow. They may have concerns for their health if it is very cold. They are afraid to venture out for fear of falling and are dependent on someone else to buy their groceries and supply other needs.

Does the Bible have anything to say about snow? Yes, there are many passages referring to snow.

Hast thou entered into the treasures of the snow: or hast thou seen the treasures of the hail.

—Job 38:22

The Bible pictures snow as a cleansing agent, refreshing and pure.

Like the coolness of snow at harvest time is a trustworthy messenger to those who send him; he refreshes the spirit of his master.

—Proverbs 25:13

The angel who rolled away the stone from the tomb of Christ is described in Matthew 28:3, "His appearance was like lightening, and his clothes were as white as snow."

In Revelation 1:14 John tells about his vision of a man. "His head and hair were white like wool, as white as snow."

But the most important contrast is in regard to the washing away of our sins.

...wash me, and I shall be whiter than snow.

—Psalm 51:7

...though your sins be as scarlet, they shall be as white as snow.

—Isaiah 1:18

What a wonderful thought! This is indeed blessed assurance.

who remembers the beautiful old song, "Whiter Than Snow"? "Now wash me, and I shall be whiter than snow."

Therefore, when we watch the snow fall as it wraps the earth in its blanket of white, think of God's love for us; think of the sacrifice Christ made for us so that we could be cleansed from our sins, washed in His blood, and emerge to a fresh, new, pure life—as white as snow.

And his raiment became shining, exceeding white as snow....
—Mark 9:3 (Transfiguration of Christ)

Praise the Lord form the earth, you great sea creatures and all ocean depths, lightening and hail, snow and clouds, stormy winds that do his bidding.
—Psalm 148:8

Sheep and Sacrifice

From the beginning of time sheep played an important part in the lives of the people of Palestine. Sheep were ceremonially clean and were therefore used in sacrifices. They were also raised for wool, meat, skins, and milk.

In the fourth chapter of Genesis we are told that Abel was a keeper of sheep. We watch through the mind's eye the family of Adam standing by the altar as Abel offers the blood sacrifice of an animal.

Abraham had large herds of animals. His descendants were shepherds when they came into Canaan after the exodus from Egyptian bondage.

Under the law of Moses, all worship centered around the various offerings and sacrifices. Once a year the sins of the people were rolled forward by animal sacrifices, but the blood of bulls and goats could never erase the people's sins permanently. Animal sacrifices were temporary and imperfect. A perfect sacrifice was possible only through a perfect Savior, and there could be no remission of sins without the shedding of blood.

In the 53rd chapter of Isaiah we read the awesome description of the coming Messiah.

Surely he took up our infirmities and carried our sorrows, yet we considered him stricken of God, smitten by him, and afflicted. But he was pierced for our transgressions, he was crushed for our iniquities; the punishment that brought us peace was upon him, and by his wounds we are healed.
We all, like sheep, have gone astray, each of us has turned to his own way; and the Lord has laid on him the iniquity of us all.
He was oppressed and afflicted, yet he did not open his mouth; he was led like

a lamb to the slaughter, and as a sheep before her shearers is silent, so he did not open his mouth.

The animal sacrifices were what man gave; the Divine Sacrifice was what God gave because he so loved the world that he gave his son.

For God so loved the world, that he gave his only begotten Son, that whosoever believed in him should not perish, but have eternal life.
—John 3:16

Just as man is destined to die once, and after that to face judgment, so Christ was sacrificed once to take away the sins of many people.
—Hebrews 9:27, 28

Under the old law the animals offered in sacrifices had to be ceremonially clean and the people had to be ceremonially clean. The laws and rules regarding sacrifices were very strict, burdensome, and difficult to comply with. Aren't you glad that we don't have to offer animal sacrifices? Christ has made the supreme sacrifice and we are under the new law of freedom and love.

Our freedom through Christ has eliminated and made obsolete the many restrictions of worship under the Mosaic law, but we have responsibilities that are not to be taken lightly.

Isn't it comforting to know that Christ is our Shepherd? He will never leave us, not during the darkest night, not in our anguish with sorrow and pain, and not even when we have sunk into the depths of sin.

The first time we meet the shepherd boy, David, who would later become king, is in I Samuel 16:11: "'There is still the youngest,' Jesse answered, 'but he is tending the sheep.'" David recognized early in his life that God was his shepherd.

The Lord is my shepherd; I shall not want.
—Psalm 23:1

David knew that sheep must have a shepherd as they are a meek and gentle animal, just as we, being spiritual sheep, need a shepherd to lead us.

It is interesting to note that angels announced the birth of Christ to shepherds tending their flocks at night. In the judgment scene, sheep are depicted as righteous people while goats are depicted as the wicked people.

And he shall set the sheep on his right hand, but the goats on the left.
—Matthew 25:33

We were lost and without hope until Christ gave himself for us and we can show gratitude by presenting our bodies as living sacrifices. Love and service are the key factors in our lives as we follow the Good Shepherd.

Therefore, I urge you, brothers in view of God's mercy, to offer your bodies as living sacrifices, holy and pleasing to God—this is your spiritual act of worship.
—Romans 12:1

With Christ as our Shepherd we must assume a different role. We must become aware of the needs of others and act accordingly.

You, my brothers, were called to be free. But do not use your freedom to indulge the sinful nature (flesh); rather, serve one another in love.
—Galatians 5:13

Your attitude should be the same as that of Christ Jesus: Who, being in the very nature God, did not consider equality with God something to be grasped, but made himself nothing taking the very nature of a servant....
—Philippians 2:5-7

To love Him with all your heart, with all your understanding and with all your strength and to love your neighbor as yourself is more important than all burnt offerings and sacrifices.
—Mark 12:33

For you were like sheep going astray, but now you have returned to the Shepherd and Overseer of your souls.
—I Peter 2:25

We may have to make sacrifices, endure hardships and suffer many things; we may have trials and tribulations, but they will be nothing in the final analysis when our Good Shepherd leads us home.

And when the Chief Shepherd appears, you will receive the crown of glory that will never fade away.
—I Peter 5:4

The Garden
of Communication

We only have to read thirty-eight verses at the beginning of Genesis to find the first garden—the Garden of Eden. God chose the beautiful setting of a garden for the home of the first man and woman.

And the Lord God planted a garden eastward in Eden; and there he put the man whom he had formed.

—Genesis 2:8

Don't you know that Adam and Eve were devastated when they were banished from the garden where they had walked and communed with God until sin forced them to leave?

Gardens represent the essence of beauty and magnificence; also calm and tranquillity. The Hanging Gardens of Babylon were one of the seven wonders of the ancient world.

Jesus sought refuge in the garden of Gethsemane to pray and meditate.

When Jesus had spoken these words, he went forth with his disciples over the brook Kidron, where was a garden, into which he entered, himself and his disciples.

—John 18:1

There in the garden Jesus was betrayed by Judas and taken prisoner. The tomb of Jesus was located in a garden. The rich man, Joseph of Arimathaea, took the body of Jesus and laid him in his own new tomb which he had hewn out of a rock (Matthew 27:57-60).

Now in the place where he was crucified there was a new tomb wherein was never man yet laid.

—John 19:41

Communication has always been important. When the world was young, in Bible times, communication was very difficult. It was necessary for people to ride donkeys or camels, or go on foot to different places to bring news and messages. These journeys took many months, and often there were people who did not learn of the death of a relative for a very long time.

When this country was settled, the Pony Express was the means by which messages were carried. Riders on horseback traveled across unsettled and dangerous territories to reach people at distant outposts.

Over the years methods of transmitting messages improved. The wireless was a breakthrough and the telephone was probably the most exciting invention of all. With the coming of radio and television the world became smaller. Now computers and fax machines make it possible to send information and communiqués everywhere in a matter of minutes. I don't have the faintest idea how these things work, but future technology may be even more astounding.

There is another area of communication that is very important: communication with friends and especially family members. We need to talk openly and honestly so that there will be no misunderstandings and so that each person can convey how he or she feels about different matters. There is nothing worse than having someone "clam up," shut everyone out, and refuse to discuss or work through situations and problems.

Often lines of communication break down between parents and children; sometimes between husbands and wives. If either of these situations exists in your life, please do everything possible to put the lines of communication back in operation.

What about our communication with God? I fear the lines are down part of the time; perhaps the lines are in need of repair.

God talks to us through his Word. He has provided a complete system of communication; nothing is lacking; nothing has been left out. Are we listening, and are we responding? He is waiting.

David was perhaps the greatest communicator of all. He talked incessantly as he pleaded for deliverance from his enemies and entreated God for forgiveness of his sins.

Answer me when I call to you, O my righteous God. Give me relief from my distress; be merciful to me and hear my prayer.

—Psalm 4:1

Daniel was in communication with God often in prayer as recorded in Daniel 9:3, "So I turned to the Lord God and pleaded with him in prayer and petition, in fasting, and in sackcloth and ashes."

Solomon prayed for wisdom and understanding; and God granted his request (1 Kings 3:5-9).

Down through the ages from the patriarchal age to the close of the New Testament, the great personages of the Bible talked, implored, and inquired through prayer to God.

The Lord is far from the wicked but he hears the prayer of the righteous.
—Proverbs 15:29

Jesus talked with his Father often and for long periods of time.

One of those days Jesus went out to a mountain side to pray, and spent the night praying to God.
—Luke 6:12

Who could forget the agonizing prayers Jesus uttered as he faced the crucifixion (Matthew 26:34-44)? And the heart rending prayer of the publican?

But the tax collector (publican) stood at a distance. He would not even look up to heaven, but beat his breast and said, 'God, have mercy on me, a sinner.'"
—Luke 18:13

Some people may be negligent in their prayer life because they don't know how to approach God's throne. They may feel that they are too insignificant or unworthy; therefore they hesitate.

And pray in the Spirit on all occasions with all kinds of prayers and requests.
—Ephesians 6:18

You need not enter a literal garden to communicate with God, but as a garden symbolizes a place of quiet and calm, you need to seek a setting of serenity in order to focus on your purpose.

If your lines of communication with God have corroded or if they are down, you need to make the repairs quickly. You have a direct line and God is waiting to hear from you.

Use it!

Gateway to Heaven

A gate is a means of entrance or exit. Let's talk about a gate for entrance. There are garden gates opening to a park or garden. There are gates to homes that are a welcoming sign if they are partially open, and there are gates to factories and places of business which permit entrance only to the people who have proper identification.

In Bible times there were many gates to Jerusalem such as the Beautiful Gate of the temple where the lame man sat. We also read about the Fish Gate, the Sheep Gate, and the Prison Gate (gate of the guard).

We talk about "the pearly gates" and because Christ gave the keys of the kingdom to Peter, many people refer to him as the keeper of the gate to heaven.

And the twelve gates were twelve pearls, each gate made of a single pearl.
—Revelation 21:21

A gate is mentioned in an incident that happened to Jacob. He was traveling toward Haran and when night approached, he took stones for his pillows and slept. He had a vision of a ladder with angels of God ascending and descending on it. When he awoke he was afraid and his thoughts are recorded in Genesis:

Surely the Lord is in this place, and I was not aware of it. He was afraid and said, 'How awesome is this place! This is none other than the house of God; this is the gate of heaven.'"

—Genesis 28:16, 17

David had some interesting thoughts on gates as recorded in the Psalms.

Enter his gates with thanksgiving and his courts with praise.

—Psalm 100:4

Open for me the gates of righteousness; I will enter and give thanks to the Lord. This is the gate of the Lord through which the righteous may enter.

—Psalm 118:19, 20

Long before the advent of Christ, Isaiah prophesied of the time when the gospel would be offered to the Gentiles as well as to the Jews.

Open the gates that the righteous nation may enter, the nation that keeps faith.

—Isaiah 26:2

An iron gate is mentioned at the time Peter was rescued from prison by the angel.

They passed the first and second guards and came to the iron gate leading to the city. It opened for them by itself, and they went through it. When they had walked the length of one street, suddenly the angel left him....

-Acts 12:10

Another gate is referred to in the crucifixion scene.

And so Jesus also suffered outside the city gate to make the people holy through his own blood.

—Hebrews 13:12

How can we gain access through the heavenly gate?

Enter through the narrow gate. For wide is the gate and broad is the road that leads to destruction, and many enter through it. But small is the gate and narrow the road that leads to life, and only a few find it.

—Matthew 7:13

I believe that this passage tells us that we have to reject the life of sin and forsake the enticements of the world that draw us away from the saving power and grace of Christ, our Savior.

Christ has paid our debt and has given us the passport to enter the gate of heaven, but in order for this passport to be valid we must accept Him through faith and obedience. As we emerge a new creature after baptism, we are given the Holy Spirit to comfort us and guide us through the Holy Word. We are also given God's grace that saves us, and, in turn, we show our love and appreciation as we live godly lives and produce good deeds.

We have to open the gates of our hearts and allow Christ to dwell within us. Then when our earthly sojourn is over, the heavenly gate will be open for us.

It had a great, high wall with twelve gates and with twelve angels at the gates. On the gates were written the names of the twelve tribes of Israel.

—Revelation 21:21

Lift up your heads, O you gates; be lifted up, you ancient doors, that the King of glory may come in. Who is this King of glory? The Lord strong and mighty, the Lord mighty in battle. Lift up your heads, O you gates; lift them up, you ancient doors, that the King of glory may come in. Who is he, this King of glory? The Lord Almighty—he is the King of glory.

—Psalm 24:7-10

Waiting in Line

All of us at one time or another have waited in lines. Many times we wait in line at the grocery, and we wait in line at the theater. There are some people who wait in lines for hours, even days, to purchase tickets to performances of their favorite country music stars.

Traffic lines are a problem and we can become impatient waiting, particularly if we are running late for an appointment. My husband used to say that all he did in the Army was hurry up and wait.

We have to wait for doctors. After reading every magazine we are still fuming and fretting as our blood pressures rise to alarming degrees.

One of the most annoying things to me is waiting for someone to pick me up to go somewhere. Being patient is one of the hardest things for me. I'm working on it, but so far not much progress has been made. It seems that all of life is a waiting game.

Some of our waiting is in pleasant anticipation of events. We wait for weddings to take place, and we wait, joyously, for the arrival of a baby. We also look forward and wait to travel and to attend family reunions.

There is another kind of waiting—waiting on God. We become impatient if our prayers are not answered the way we had hoped, but God in his infinite wisdom may be saying, "Wait."

Rest in the Lord and wait patiently for Him.

—Psalm 37:7

When we have suffered an injustice and may want to seek revenge, we must wait.

For the Lord is a God of justice. Blessed are those who wait for Him!
—Isaiah 30:18

Have you ever felt hopeless? Maybe you are in a situation in which you feel all hope is gone; you do not see a glimmer of hope and no light at the end of the tunnel.

I wait for the Lord, my soul waits, and in his word I put my hope. My soul waits for the Lord more than watchmen wait for the morning.
—Psalm 130:5-6

Just as there are many kinds of waiting in the physical world, there are various kinds of waiting in the spiritual sphere. We read in the book of Mark that Joseph of Arimathea was waiting for the kingdom of God.

...Joseph of Arimathea, a prominent member of the Council, who was himself waiting for the kingdom of God, went boldly to Pilate and asked for Jesus' body.

—Mark 15:43

Shortly before the ascension, Christ instructed his disciples to wait for the Holy Spirit to come.

Do not leave Jerusalem, but wait for the gift my Father promised, which you have heard me speak about.

—Acts 1:4

The Holy Word admonishes us to wait for our adoption as children of God and to await righteousness.

But we ourselves, who have the first fruits of the Spirit, groan inwardly as we wait eagerly for our adoption as sons, the redemption of our bodies.

—Romans 8:23

But by faith we eagerly await through the Spirit the righteousness for which we hope.

—Galatians 5:5

The most important event that we should wait for with anticipation is the coming of our Savior to take us to our permanent home prepared for us.

And to wait for his Son from heaven, whom he raised from the dead, even Jesus, which delivered us from the wrath to come.

—I Thessalonians 1:10

He who testifies to these things says, "Yes, I am coming soon." Amen. Come, Lord Jesus.

—Revelation 22:20

In hope, trust and faith we wait.
Wait on the Lord!

Under the Fig Tree

Do you like figs? In the yard of my home in Jackson, Tennessee, was a large fig tree, and as August approached we eagerly awaited the appearance of the ripe figs. The leaves were large and beautiful, and as the small green figs began to develop it seems forever before they ripened. My mother made fig preserves which were very good, but I enjoyed eating the figs off the tree.

The fig trees in Palestine are taller than the ones in this country. They grow to a height of fifteen feet and are very prolific. Figs were very prominent and important in Bible times. The first clothing was fig leaves; figs were a staple food and were also used for medicinal purposes. When Hezekiah was sick, he asked God to lengthen his life.

And Isaiah said, "Take a lump of figs." And they took and laid it on the boil, and he recovered.

—II Kings 20:7

The fig tree was a symbol of safety and peaceful living.

During Solomon's lifetime Judah and Israel, from Dan to Beersha, lived in safety, each man under his own vine and fig tree.

—I Kings 4:25

The prophecy of the coming of the Messiah and the glory and victory of the church was represented by the vine and the fig tree.

...Nation will not take up sword against nation, nor will they train for war anymore. Every man will sit under his own vine and under his own fig tree, and no one will make them afraid, for the Lord Almighty has spoken.

—Micah 4:3, 4

All of us desire peace and safety in our lives. Safety is a great concern today due to so much crime and violence. We need to be alert in every situation so as not to become a victim. Peace is hard to attain also; there is strife and turmoil on every hand, even in families.

Where can we find peace and safety?

...but whoever trusts in the Lord is kept safe.

—Proverbs 29:25

Therefore, if we trust in God, he has promised that we will be safe.

Peace I leave with you; my peace I give you. I do not give to you as the world gives. Do not let your hearts be troubled and so not be afraid.

—John 14:27

Jesus told us not to worry because he has given us his peace, and in this next passage he said that we will have peace in Him.

I have told you these things, so that in me you may have peace.

—John 16:33

When we have been justified through faith, we will have peace.

Therefore, since we have been justified through faith, we will have peace with God through our Lord, Jesus Christ.

—Romans 5:1

Do not be anxious about anything, but in everything, by prayer and petition, with thanksgiving, present your requests to God. And the peace of God which transcends all understanding, will guard your hearts and your minds in Christ Jesus.

—Philippians 4:6, 7

The main ingredients are trust, faith, prayer; and I Timothy 2:2 tells us how to live peaceful and quiet lives.

I urge, then, first of all, that requests, prayers, intercession and thanksgiving be made for everyone—for kings and all those in authority, that we may live peaceful and quiet lives in all godliness and holiness.

Since we have the assurance that through trust in God, we will have safety, and because Christ has left his peace with us through our faith, then, in full confidence, we can enjoy sitting under our own fig tree.

Promises! Promises!

When you were a child did you ever say to someone, "I promise; cross my heart and hope to die"? Perhaps it was a promise to keep a deep, dark secret.

Parents make promises to their children, "I promise to take you to the zoo next week." Children may promise their parents, "I promise to work harder in order to make better grades."

We listen as a happy couple, in a wedding ceremony, promise to love, honor, and cherish one another until parted by death. Tragically, many of these vows are broken resulting in disappointment and disillusionment.

Promises are not to be taken lightly. We should not promise anything unless we are reasonably sure that we will be able to comply. Unfortunately, some people make promises knowing that they won't or can't keep them. One such group are the politicians who make campaign promises that are seldom kept.

Keeping promises is a matter of integrity, and we should teach our children and grandchildren the seriousness of fulfilling what they have promised.

We may be disappointed by friends, relatives, children, persons in authority and high places who have broken promises, but there is one source that we can count on without fail: God's promises are steadfast and sure, never failing.

What do you think about when you see a rainbow? I think it is very thrilling to see a rainbow, not only for its beauty, but for the promise God made.

...Never again will the waters become a flood to destroy all life. Whenever the rainbow appears in the clouds, I will see it and will remember the everlasting covenant between God and all living creatures of every kind on the earth. So God said to Noah, "This is the sign of the covenant I have established between me and all life on earth.

—Genesis 9:15-17

On that day God made a covenant with Abram and said, "To your descendants I give this land, from the river of Egypt to the great river, the Euphrates.

—Genesis 15:18

This was the first land grant that was made by God to Abraham and his descendants. God kept this promise although the children of Israel complained regularly and were often unfaithful. God promised them manna and quail as they traveled through the desert towards Canaan, and this food was provided by God until they reached the land flowing with milk and honey.

When the temple was completed under the direction of Solomon, he brought the people together for a solemn dedication and blessed the entire assembly of Israel.

Praise be to the Lord, who has given rest to his people Israel just as he promised. Not one word has failed of all the good promises he gave through his servant Moses.

—I Kings 8:56

Now, let's go to the New Testament to discover some of God's promises. Jesus gave his disciples final instruction before his ascension in Luke 24:49:

I am going to send you what my Father has promised; but stay in the city until you have been clothed with power from on high.

This refers to the promise of the Holy Spirit who would bring comfort to the disciples after the departure of Christ. This same Spirit is with us as God's children to comfort us until Christ comes back to claim his won.

Eternal rest is promised to the faithful as recorded in Hebrews 4:1:

Therefore, since the promise of entering His rest still stands, let us be careful that none of you be found to have fallen short of it.

From Genesis to Revelation the scriptures are filled with God's promises, therefore, we have the assurance that He will strengthen us when we are weak; He will comfort us when we are grieved; He will give us refuge and rest when we are weary. Through faith and by His grace, He will give us salvation with the blessed promise of an eternal home which is being prepared at this very moment.

He gives strength to the weary and increases the power of the weak.

—Isaiah 40:29

Even though I walk through the valley of the shadow of death, I will fear no evil for you are with me; your rod and your staff, they comfort me.

—Psalm 23:4

...there the weary will be at rest.
—Job 3:17 (Reference is of heaven.)

Blessed are those who mourn, for they will be comforted.
—Matthew 5:4

God is our refuge and strength, a very present help in trouble.
—Psalm 46:1

I will say of the Lord, He is my refuge and my fortress....
—Psalm 91:2

God has kept his promises since the beginning of time and through the ages; and He always will.
You can count on it!

The Fountain of Life

Do you like fountains? Children do. Have you ever noticed the actions of young children when they see a fountain? Some run excitedly to either throw a coin in the fountain or to put their hands in the water. Other children just stand and watch in awe as the water rises and falls in the never ending cascade shooting upward.

Fountains are found in many places: parks, gardens, elegant hotels, and even malls. Many public buildings have fountains inside as well as outside, and what could be more beautiful than a fountain in front of a palatial home. I like to think that the Garden of Eden had a fountain to add beauty to that perfect setting.

What about the fountain of life? What is it? How can we find this fountain, and where do we start? Let's look in the Holy Word; first in Proverbs 13:14: "The teaching of the wise is a fountain of life." Proverbs 18:4 says: "...the fountain of wisdom is a bubbling brook."

The Scriptures tell us, don't they? Wisdom has something to do with the fountain of life.

> *How much better to get wisdom than gold! To choose understanding rather than silver!*
> —Proverbs 16:16

> *...wisdom brightens a man's face and changes its hard appearance.*
> —Ecclesiastes 8:1

For some reason many people feel that wisdom is elusive, that some people are just naturally wiser than others. We need to have the desire for wisdom to the extent that we are willing to study and make application in our lives.

> *Get wisdom, get understanding; do not forget my words or swerve from them. Do not forsake wisdom and she will protect you; love her, and she will watch over you. Wisdom is supreme; therefore, get wisdom.*
> —Proverbs 4:5-7

The more we read and study God's word, the more we will want to discover the unsearchable riches contained in the Holy Word. There is nothing dull or boring about the Bible. It is the most exciting book ever written but most importantly it contains the words of life—eternal life.

It is necessary to have a plan of study. Set aside a certain time of day to read and study. Make notes; read and re-read. We cannot afford to neglect the reading of God's word.

If any of you lacks wisdom, he should ask God, who gives generously to all without finding fault, and it will be given to him. But when he asks, he must believe and not doubt, because he who doubts is like a wave of the sea, blown and tossed by the wind.

—James 1:5, 6, 7

There is another source of the fountain of life—the main source.

For with you (God) is the fountain of life.

—Psalm 36:9

...they have forsaken me the fountain of living water.

—Jeremiah 17:13

For the Lamb at the center of the throne will be their shepherd; He will lead them to springs (fountains) of living water. And God will wipe away every tear from their eyes.

—Revelation 7:17

...I am Alpha and Omega, the beginning and the end. I will give unto him that is athirst of the fountain of the water of life freely.

—Revelation 21:6

Now, we know how to obtain the fountain of life. Through diligent study of God's word we will gain wisdom. Then by surrender to Christ, our Savior, and with Him as our guide, He will lead us to the fountain of living water.

For with you is the fountain of life.

—Psalm 36:9

God's Dress Code

Clothes are very important to some people; they want to wear the latest styles to be with the "in" group or to make a statement. There is a saying, "clothes make the man," but that is a false concept, of course. Then there's "the man of distinction," always elegantly dressed in the advertisements.

On the other hand, the poor are not concerned with the latest styles, but they are desirous of necessary clothing. I believe that most people want to look nice and attractive, not flashy and ostentatious.

Now we come to the group who have gone in an entirely different direction. Their clothing seems to consist mainly of blue jeans with sloppy shirts and sweaters; not because they don't have anything better, but they, too, are trying to make some kind of statement. Perhaps it is rebellion against the establishment and tradition. Sometimes this group appears everywhere in their slovenly looking clothes.

There is no doubt that we can place too much emphasis on our clothing, especially if we feel that everything has to be the finest and the most expensive. However, it is possible to be too casual and not give the proper attention to our clothing.

I'm very concerned about personal appearance at worship services. We must enter the presence of God with respect, awe, and reverence. How do we show proper respect?—by having the proper attitude of heart and mind, and by being dressed neatly.

I'm sure we wouldn't go on a job interview in sloppy attire; neither would we go to a wedding looking like we just came off the ball field. If we were invited to the White House we would want to look our best. Why? Out of respect and decorum. So it is doubly important that we come before God with proper respect.

I am not referring to people who do not have nice clothes; we should never put them down if they come to worship wearing the best they have.

The Lord does not look at the things man looks at. Man looks at the outward appearance, but the Lord looks at the heart.
—I Samuel 16:7

It may be that some people feel that we in the church have become too formal, too ritualistic, and too traditional. Therefore, they have taken a counter-active measure in the form of their dress.

It may be true that we need to examine several areas and make sure that we have not become too traditional, but at the same time we must remember the object of our worship, making sure that we come before God suitably and respectfully attired.

In I Timothy women are admonished to dress with decency and propriety. This means not dressed carelessly, slovenly, or elaborately.

I also want women to dress modestly, with decency and propriety, not with braided hair or gold or pearls or expensive clothes, but with good deeds, appropriate for women who profess to worship God.

All of us must be concerned about the spiritual clothing we are wearing.

I put on righteousness as my clothing; justice was my robe and my turban.
—Job 29:14

All of you, clothe yourselves with humility toward one another, because God opposes the proud but give grace to the humble.
—I Peter 5:5

Now we have discovered that God looks at the heart, not the outward appearance and that we are to clothe ourselves in good deeds, righteousness, humility, and justice. At the same time we must not dress too casually with no thought at all about our appearance, neither should we dress so elegantly and elaborately that we call attention to ourselves. We must remember the reason for our assembling in the place of worship. Just as in most things, there is a happy medium.

Let all things be done decently and in order.
—I Corinthians 14:40

Before going to worship we need to program our minds and prepare our hearts in readiness to offer praises and adoration to our Heavenly Father. We want our worship to be pleasing to God and, in order for all things to be acceptable, we must worship in spirit and in truth. Also we need to dress appropriately.

Yes, God does have a dress code!

Wings of Eagles

What do you think Adam thought when he saw the first bird flying in the sky? Do you wonder what kind of bird it was? I do. Was it a small bird such as a sparrow, or was it a hummingbird sipping nectar from the flowers in the Garden of Eden?

Could it have been a large bird such as the eagle? The first mention of birds flying about the earth is recorded in Genesis 1:20, but the account fails to tell us what kind of birds were created first.

Man has been fascinated with the idea of flying since the beginning of time, and finally, after trial and error, and endless experiments, the airplane was invented. At last, like the eagle spreading its massive wings, a man-made machine with wings of mammoth proportions, was ready for man to soar through the heavens.

As we look at old film clips of the Wright brothers experimenting with their planes, we are amused at the rather crude efforts, but it was a beginning. It is my understanding that they studied the eagle in order to gain some knowledge of flight.

Eagles are known for keenness of vision and powers of flight. There was an ancient belief that after a certain period the eagle renewed its youth.

In Proverbs 30:19, Solomon said one of the wonderful things for him was: "The way of an eagle in the air."

The eagle is a symbol for the United States of America because of its swiftness, its vision, and the mighty expanse of its wings. It appears as a logo on mail trucks and priority mail.

Is there a relevance for us in the study of wings and eagles?

Ye have seen what I did unto the Egyptians, and how I bare you on eagles' wings and brought you unto myself.

—Exodus 19:4

Wings are symbolic of refuge, healing and strength.

Both high and low among men find refuge in the shadow of your wings.

—Psalm 36:7

In this passage David writes that God provides refuge for us beneath His wings.

We are admonished not to trust in riches because they can fly away.

Cast but a glance at riches, and they are gone, for they will surely sprout wings and fly off to the sky like an eagle.

—Proverbs 23:5

God cares for us at all times and under all circumstances, and the beautiful symbol of His wings providing this care should be a constant reminder for us and bring great comfort.

But those who hope in the Lord will renew their strength. They will soar on wings of eagles. They will run and not grow weary, they will walk and not be faint.

—Isaiah 40:31

But for you who revere my name, the sun of righteousness will rise with healing in its wings.

—Malachi 4:2

Jesus wanted to gather the people of Jerusalem under his wings, but they refused. His lament is recorded in Matthew 23:37:

O Jerusalem, Jerusalem, you who kill the prophets and stone those sent to you, how often I have longed to gather your children together, as a hen gathers her chicks under her wings, but you were not willing.

All of us want to feel protected and secure. God has used the symbol of the mighty wings of eagles to show us how powerful and caring He is, if we will seek shelter beneath His wings.

If I rise on the wings of the dawn, if I settle on the far side of the sea, even there your hand will guide me, your right hand will hold me fast.

—Psalm 139:9

Do you like the song, "I'll Fly Away?" I do.

While here traveling the pilgrim pathway, we have the security, protection, healing, and refuge beneath the wings of God; then at last, when it is time for our earthly life to close, we will fly away like the eagles that soar above the earth. God will bear us on his mighty wings.

Some glad morning when this life is o'er, I'll fly away
To a home on God's celestial shore, I'll fly away.

The Puzzling Puzzle

Do you like jigsaw puzzles? My first one had four or five pieces which at the time was a real challenge. As I got older the puzzles contained more pieces, and they were much smaller.

The last puzzle I tackled was several years ago. As I dumped the 1000 pieces on the table, I had the feeling it would never be completed. The pieces were so small and so many were the same color, making it almost impossible to determine where they were supposed to be placed. After the initial hesitation I became determined to complete it.

Did you every play "Let's Pretend"? You pretended to be someone else or something else. Let's play again. This time let's pretend that your body is a puzzle. Our bodies are made up of many different parts, and each part has its own function.

The body is a unit, though it is made up of many parts; and though all its parts are many, they form one body. So it is with Christ....Now the body is not made up of one part but of many.
—I Corinthians 12:12-14

The eye cannot do the work of the ear, and the hand can not function as the foot. Only when each part does what it was designed to do is the puzzle of our body complete.

Now, let's pretend that the spiritual body (the church) is a puzzle.

Now you are the body of Christ, and each one of you is a part of it.
—I Corinthians 12:27

Each person in the church (the body of Christ) has a function but not the same function. For the puzzle pieces to fit in their proper places, we must recognize our own particular function.

Some people are preachers, some are teachers, some are elders while others minister to the needy, encourage the distressed, and exhort the weak. Everyone has a responsibility and everyone must recognize and accept his limitations.

Some positions are more prominent than others, nevertheless, each duty is important and has a special purpose. The puzzle pieces will not fit unless we acknowledge the fact that each piece has its particular niche.

The quiet, unassuming person, who is daily writing notes of encouragement and performing many deeds in an inconspicuous way, may be accomplishing more than the person in a more prominent position.

There are some women who feel that they are being cheated because they cannot participate in some or all of the more prominent services of the church. Why is this? Women have a very important and unique place in the church teaching their children and other people's children. The influence of a godly woman plus the training and teaching provided to family members has produced many outstanding preachers. Many men acknowledge the fact that they owe everything to the instruction and guidance of their mothers. What could be more important than this?

....the woman is the glory of man.

—I Corinthians 11:7

A virtuous woman is a crown to her husband.

—Proverbs 12:4

A wife of noble character who can find? She is worth far more than rubies. Her husband has full confidence in her and lacks nothing of value. She brings him good, not harm, all the days of her life.

—Proverbs 31:10-12

I do not permit a woman to teach or to have authority over a man; she must be silent.

—I Timothy 2:12

A woman should not be intimidated by this passage, but gracefully accept her role which is so special, unique and powerful.

Whether you are old or young, rich or poor, male or female, you have a specific and valuable place in the church. Only when each person recognizes his own special work will the pieces fit into the right place so that the puzzle of life will be complete and whole.

Once Upon a Frosty Morn

I like to witness the birth of each new day. Sometimes I miss it because of oversleeping, but I always anticipate the glories of the early morning. Each day is different in its birth. Some aspects are the same, but if you observe closely you will be rewarded with a serendipity.

As I drew the blinds this morning I wondered what would be the surprise, if any. I also like to contemplate what the day will bring forth. We never know, do we?

At first, I thought a light snow was on the ground, but Jack Frost had paid a visit and his minute ice crystals had carpeted the ground. The bare branches of the trees stood out in sharp contrast with the frost. A few billowy clouds were in the sky, mostly pale pink and blue. I could almost see them move as they floated majestically across the sky. The sun began to make its appearance slowly hugging the eastern horizon, trying to decide whether or not to shine today. Finally, in all its glory and force it showed its brilliancy. Then, suddenly, it decided to play peek-a-boo like a playful child.

How can anyone doubt that there is a God, *the God* and *the Creator* of living things, who has surrounded us with so much beauty for us to enjoy as we sojourn on this earth?

A few moments of quiet reflection each morning and taking time to view the glories of nature that surround us will equip us with a resiliency to face the tasks and problems of the day.

Try it! You might like it.

O Lord, our Lord, how majestic is your name in all the earth! You have set your glory above the heavens.

—Psalm 8:1

Does the rain have a father? Who fathers the drops of dew? From whose womb comes the ice? Who gives birth to the frost from the heavens when the waters become hard as stone, when the surface of the deep is frozen?

—Job 38:28-30

He covers the sky with clouds....

—Psalm 147:8

He spreads the snow like wool and scatters the frost like ashes.

—Psalm 147:16

The Unkindest Cut of All

When I was five years old our next door neighbors had a boy of five who was my playmate. He had a birthday party, and I was very excited because it was to be my first. He and his mother stood at the door to greet the children, and each time he was handed a gift he said, "Thank you ever and ever so much." This expression of gratitude stayed in my memory, and, even though it has been over seventy years, it is still very vivid.

One of the first things parents teach small children is to say, "Thank you." Perhaps it has become second nature with most of us, a fact which causes me to wonder if we really mean it every time we say, "Thank you."

For some reason, it is hard for some people to say, "Thank you." At least this has been my experience. Have they not been taught, or do they feel uncomfortable expressing thanks?

Thanksgiving is a special holiday when people seem to be especially grateful. Many poems and articles are written on the subject, and we sing songs of grateful praise more during this particular holiday season. But what about the remainder of the year?

Enter his gates with thanksgiving and his courts with praise; give thanks to Him and praise His name.

—Psalm 100:4

Often our lives are filled with complaints. Things never seem to be exactly right. It is either too hot or too cold; things move too quickly or too slowly; people are not friendly enough or they ask too many questions. Where is the spirit of thanksgiving and the gift of gratitude?

All this is for your benefit, so that the grace that is reaching more and more people may cause thanksgiving to overflow to the glory of God.

-II Corinthians 4:15

Regardless of our circumstances we have much to be thankful for. Ingratitude is an ugly word, and we must not be guilty of it, especially in regard to the innumerable gifts and blessings that God has showered upon us.

Are we thankful enough for grace? Do we really understand what it means to have God's grace? Christ redeemed us by his blood, sacrificing his life so that we may have grace, which is unmerited and undeserved favor, sustenance and help. In every prayer we should express thanks for God's grace.

Thanks be to God for his indescribable gift. (grace)
—II Corinthians 9:15

We have not done anything to merit God's grace, neither can we do anything to earn grace. We do not collect "Brownie Points" or mark x's on the calendar in order to receive grace. It is freely given to us by our Savior.

We should enter the house of worship in the spirit of thanksgiving.

Sing and make music in your heart to the Lord, always giving thanks to God the Father for everything, in the name of our Lord Jesus Christ.
—Ephesians 5:19, 20

But thanks be to God! He gives us the victory through our Lord Jesus Christ.
—I Corinthians 15:57

Most of us have a prayer list of names that we present to God daily. Let's also have a list of things for which we are grateful.

The list should grow and grow as we begin to contemplate our blessings. Don't let a day pass without expressing thanks to your family and friends. Don't wait too late to show gratitude for kindnesses shown or good deeds done. Don't thank God in general terms for His blessings, but name them one by one as the song expresses it.

And God raised us up with Christ and seated us with him in the heavenly realms in Christ Jesus, in order that in the coming ages he might show the incomparable riches of his grace, expressed in his kindness to us in Christ Jesus.

—Ephesians 2:6

Don't be guilty of ingratitude—the unkindest cut of all!

Every good and perfect gift is from above, coming down from the Father of the heavenly lights, who does not change like shifting shadows. He chose to give us birth through the word of truth, that we might be a kind of firstfruits of all he created.

—James 1:17

Commitment Failure

All of us have commitments of one kind or another. What are you committed to? You should be committed to your marriage and to your job; perhaps to a certain cause and particular people. Has there ever been a breakdown in these pledges? Has failure resulted?

First, let us look at examples in the Bible of men who remained steadfast to their commitment under unusual circumstances, and even threats of death.

God came to Moses in the burning bush and commissioned him to lead the children of Israel out of Egyptian bondage. At first Moses made excuses but when God persuaded him, he became fully committed to the task (Exodus 3).

Faith is a prerequisite to commitment and this is brought out in Hebrews 11:24-26:

> *By faith, Moses, when he was grown up, refused to be known as the son of Pharaoh's daughter. He chose to be mistreated along with the people of God rather than enjoy the pleasures of sin for a short time. He regarded disgrace for the sake of Christ as of greater value than the treasures of Egypt, because he was looking ahead to his reward.*

When the young man, Daniel, was a captive in Babylon and was singled out for special service to the king, he refused to partake of the royal food and wine because he was committed to God.

> *But Daniel resolved not to defile himself with the royal food and wine, and he asked the chief official for permission not to defile himself this way.*
> —Daniel 1:8

Later King Darius issued a decree stating that for thirty days no one was to pray to any god but him. This decree was made at the urging of the king's administrators, but, again, Daniel defied the order.

> *Now when Daniel learned that the decree had been published, he went home to his upstairs room where the windows opened toward Jerusalem. Three times a day he got down on his knees and prayed, giving thanks to God, just as he had done before.*
> —Daniel 6:10

Because of his violation of the decree, Daniel was thrown into the lions' den, but we know that God rescued him because he was committed to faithfulness.

I'm sure you remember the story of Esther, wife of Xerxes (Ahasureus), and how she came to be queen. This account of events is filled with intrigue, suspense, and danger.

Esther's uncle, Mordecai, pleaded with her to assist in saving the Jews.

For if you remain silent at this time, relief and deliverance for the Jews will arise from another place, but you and your father's family will perish. And who knows but that you have come to royal position for such a time as this?
—Esther 4:14

Esther could have been banished or put to death for appearing before the king without being summoned, but she did not hesitate to commit herself to the task and said: "...I will go to the king, even though it is against the law. And if I perish, I perish."

What courage this must have taken; what thoughts must have run through her mind as she approached the king.

We move to the New Testament to the first Christian martyr. Stephen is an example of boldness and total commitment to the cause of Christ, and for this he was falsely accused of blasphemy and stoned to death. His commitment was complete and unwavering even to the point of praying that his murderers would be forgiven (Acts 6).

The apostle, Paul, was probably the most committed person in the Bible. When we meet him he is known as Saul, and he was persecuting the Lord's disciples and the church. After his unusual conversion, he became totally committed to Christ and established churches in what is known today as Turkey, Greece, and Italy. He wrote at least thirteen letters of Scripture and suffered persecution more than any other person, but he never wavered in his conviction even though he was arrested many times and spent a number of years in prison.

For which cause I suffer also these things: yet I am not ashamed; for I know him whom I have believed, and I am persuaded that he is able to guard that which I have committed unto him against that day.
—II Timothy 1:12

What about commitments in today's world? Often commitments are not taken seriously. Jobs are taken lightly, even marriages. A lack

100

of morals in today's society and attitudes of selfishness and uncaring have produced failures of dedication and devotion. Divorce is rampant and taken lightly. Some enter marriage with the idea that if it doesn't work, "it's no big deal," and they can easily get out of the situation.

A lack of commitment in the earthly realm is bad enough, but it is devastating in the spiritual sphere. It is necessary to be completely committed to Christ in order to be pleasing to God. We can't be wishy-washy, half-hearted, Sunday morning Christians; if so, there will be failure in all aspects of our lives.

> *I know your deeds, that you are neither cold nor hot. I wish you were either one or the other! So, because you are lukewarm—neither hot nor cold—I am about to spit you out of my mouth.*
> —Revelation 3:15-16 (To the church in Laodicea)

This was a very serious charge to that church and we don't want to be guilty of the same thing. We cannot afford to be lukewarm; we must not have commitment failure.

Lighthouse of Hope

Have you ever been to the top of a lighthouse and pretended that you were the keeper, flashing the beams and signals on a dark and stormy night? In your mind's eye you would feel so heroic as you pictured a ship at sea, in turbulent waters and unsure of its course until the beams you had set in motion gave direction.

The ancient Egyptians built the first lighthouse, the tallest ever constructed. Much later the Romans built towers at a number of ports.

The first lighthouse in America was in Boston Harbor. The British destroyed it in 1776 during the Revolutionary War, but another was built on the same site in 1783, and it still stands.

Lighthouses were built in harbors, on capes, and peninsulas, and even in the sea. In the Florida Keys there is one whose metal stilts are screwed into the floor of the sea.

Until the 1940's lighthouses were indispensable for navigation on the seas. At the time, advancement in electronic technology eliminated the necessity for many or most of the lighthouses.

As lighthouses were the only source of hope and safety in earlier times, we need a spiritual lighthouse so that we can have hope and security.

What is hope? It is desire accompanied by expectation or belief of fulfillment. We hope for many things. We hope that our children will succeed and that they will be faithful Christians. We hope that we can maintain good health and that the plans we have made will materialize. Farmers hope that their crops will survive either flood or drought, and that they will have a good harvest.

What about spiritual hope? Do you really feel that you have hope of eternal life? Many people say, "I hope I will be saved," but the tone of their voices indicates that they aren't sure. Do you have the expectation that God will take care of you in all situations? Do you trust in God so completely that you know He will answer your prayers?

...a faith and knowledge resting on the hope of eternal life, which God, who does not lie, promised before the beginning of time.
—Titus 1:1-2

We are told in this passage that God promised us eternal life before the world was made and that this hope is built on faith and knowledge. Faith provides us with an anchor of hope.

For in hope were we saved.
—Romans 8:24

Which hope we have as an anchor of the soul, both sure and steadfast.
—Hebrews 6:19

For we through the Spirit wait for the hope of righteousness by faith.
—Galatians 5:5

Just as the keeper of the lighthouse watches for ships that may be lost in unfamiliar waters, we are admonished to watch in hope.

But as for me I watch in hope for the Lord, I wait for God, my Savior, my God will hear me.

In times of need, distress and helplessness, the only sure place to go is to God.

We wait in hope for the Lord, he is our help and our shield.
—Psalm 33:20

...Put your hope in God, for I will yet praise him, my Savior and my God.
—Psalm 42:11

We know that God is in His lighthouse sending beams of light to guide us to safety. We may be tossed to and fro in uncertainty, anxiety and despair, but God is there to draw us to a safe haven where we will be protected from all harm.

We used to sing:

Brightly beams our Father's mercy
From His lighthouse evermore,
But to us He gives the keeping
Of the lights along the shore.

Isn't it comforting to have the assurance and the hope that God is continually watching over us?

This is a trustworthy saying that deserves full acceptance (and for this we labor and strive) that we have put our hope in the living God, who is the Savior of all men, especially of those who believe.

—I Timothy 4:9, 10

The Circle of Mercy

"Circle the wagons, circle the wagons!" was the cry of the settlers trekking across the deserted western territory. This shout gave notice of impending danger; most likely from Indians spotted on a pinnacle overlooking the people in their covered wagon procession. If the circle was enclosed quickly the settlers were able, sometimes, to ward off the Indians.

A circle has different functions, such as a boundary. When playing some games it is necessary to stay within the circle. As a child I enjoyed playing marbles and the first thing that had to be done was to draw a circle on the ground.

On the other hand, I disliked games that required a person to be in the middle of the circle. I didn't want to be that person because I was very shy. Another uncomfortable position for me would be in the center of a spotlight with a big, round circle of light focusing on me.

A circle has another connotation, that is, an unending quality. It is impossible to determine where a circle begins and where it ends. For this reason, it is a symbol of unending love and is expressed this way in many marriage ceremonies.

The circle denotes wholeness and completeness. We speak of the family circle and a circle of friends. It has the feeling of protection—a haven and a refuge.

Now, let's change course and talk about another circle—the circle of God's mercy. The very sound of the word mercy alludes to compassion. It is not only compassion but pity and leniency—a special favor even to those who are undeserving of mercy. Many of us have heard the story of the man standing before the judge and trembling. The judge says, "Don't be afraid, you will receive justice in my court." The man still trembling replies, "Judge, what I need is mercy."

All of us are in this situation. We need mercy—we need God's mercy

...while we were yet sinners, Christ died for us.
—Romans 5:8

In mercy and compassion and love Christ gave his life for us.

His mercy is endless, all enduring, and all encompassing, but we have to be repentant. We cannot continue to be obstinate and rebellious and expect mercy. We have to pay the penalty for sin and suffer the consequences for wrong doing, but the penalty is not a life sentence, if we are willing to change.

His mercy extends to those who fear him, from generation to generation.
—Luke 1:50

The Lord is slow to anger, abounding in love and forgiving sin and rebellion. Yet he does not leave the guilty unpunished.
—Numbers 14:18

Throughout the history of God's chosen people, the Israelites were rebellious and disobedient. They were tempted by the people around them to worship idols and participate in other abominable practices. They soon forgot the dividing of the Red Sea and their deliverance from the Egyptians, and they forgot the manna and the quail.

The Lord our God is merciful and forgiving, even though we have rebelled against him...
—Daniel 9:9

When the nation was divided into two kingdoms, Judah and Israel, the people continued to worship idols. God admonished them constantly through the prophets, but usually their return was short lived.

"Return, faithless Israel," declares the Lord, "I will frown on you no longer, for I am merciful," declares the Lord, "I will not be angry forever. Only acknowledge your guilt."
—Jeremiah 3:12

The Egyptian bondage was due to sin and disobedience but ended when Moses led the Israelites to Canaan, the promised land. Because the people slipped back into their old habits and forgot God, they were confronted, once again, with bondage. Israel was captured by Assyria, and Judah was subdued three times; first, by Nebuchadnezzar, then by the Babylonians, and finally, Jerusalem fell. The city was destroyed and the inhabitants carried away; however, God promised their release which took place in 536 B.C. under Cyrus.

God talked with Jeremiah about the unfaithfulness of Judah and Israel and predicted their bondage.

"Yet even in those days," declares the Lord, "I will not destroy you completely. And when the people ask, 'Why has the Lord done this to us?' you will tell them, 'As you have forsaken me and served foreign gods in your own land, so now you will serve foreigners in a land not your own.'"
　　　　　　　　　　　　　　　　　　　　　　　　—Jeremiah 5:18-19

Therefore this is what the Sovereign Lord says: "My anger and my wrath will be poured out on this place, on man and beast, on the trees of the fields and on the fruit of the ground, and it will burn and not be quenched."
　　　　　　　　　　　　　　　　　　　　　　　　—Jeremiah 7:20

David felt his inadequacy and need for God's mercy, and he pleaded in anguish, but his cries were always made in a penitent spirit and complete submission.

Let thy mercy, O Lord, be upon us, according as we hope in thee.
　　　　　　　　　　　　　　　　　　　　　　　　—Psalm 33:22

Have mercy on me, O Lord, according to your unfailing love; according to your great compassion blot out my transgressions.
　　　　　　　　　　　　　　　　　　　　　　　　—Psalm 51:1

All of us are saturated with our humanity and it is a constant battle between the flesh and the spirit. We cannot go our own way, do things our way and disregard God's truths and expect mercy.

Hear my prayer, O Lord; listen to my cry for mercy. In the day of my trouble I will call to you, for you will answer me.
　　　　　　　　　　　　　　　　　　　　　　　　—Psalm 86:6, 7

God is sad when we sin and are not repentant; he is sad when we forsake Him, or become lukewarm, complacent, and slothful; but we know that if we come to Him trusting, believing, hoping, and stricken with our shortcomings to the point of crying, "Please forgive," that His love and mercy will surround us and enclose us in the unending circle of His mercy.

Let us approach the throne of grace with confidence, so that we may receive mercy and grace to help us in our time of need.
　　　　　　　　　　　　　　　　　　　　　　　　—Hebrews 4:16

Blessed be God, even the Father of our Lord Jesus Christ, the Father of mercies, and the God of all comfort.
　　　　　　　　　　　　　　　　　　　　　　　　—II Corinthians 1:3

Sounds and Storms

What do we think of when we hear the word "sound"? If used as a noun we would think of noise, vibration, and reverberation; but if used as an adjective we would think of "sound" as something valid, legal, or orthodox. We talk about sound minds and sound bodies which means healthy and whole.

There are discussions now about different sounds. What is meant by "different"? Different means not of the same kind, but does that mean that if something is not of the same kind that it is necessarily not sound or valid?

Most of us don't like to alter things. We are happy with the status quo, the way situations have always been, and we don't want to be different or unconventional. Old habits, set routines, and rigid schedules are very hard to break, but if we came to the realization that our lives had become stagnant and inactive and if we thought that some of our attitudes needed adjustment, would we be willing to undergo transformation? If so, where would we start?

Before we answer that question let's think about the word "storm." It immediately sets fear in motion. I have never experienced a hurricane or an earthquake, and I hope I never do, but I have been in the midst of two snow storms, and in both instances the snow was so heavy that the road was invisible and the signs disguised with snow. I have lived through two ice storms in which extensive damage was done. Therefore, the word "storm" incites apprehension.

There are different kinds of storms—storms of life. All of us come face to face with them sooner or later. Illness, death, failure, disappointment, and betrayal stir up the turbulent waters and produce storms in our lives, but we have an advocate to help us in these kinds of storms.

You have been a refuge for the poor, a refuge for the needy in his distress, a shelter from the storm and a shade from the heat.

—Isaiah 25:4

Throughout the religious world, we hear rumblings of storms brewing; we are told that different sounds are vibrating. What does this signify? Many people are confused and disturbed, and what should we, as individual Christians, do if anything?

Once again, I urge you to allow the Holy Spirit, through His word, to guide you into all truth.

And ye shall know the truth and the truth shall make you free.
—John 8:32

Jesus answered, "I am the way and the truth and the life. No one comes to the Father except through me." (Jesus answering Thomas)
—John 14:6

Since Jesus is the truth and the way, we must determine what his commandments are. We will place Christ center-front as the focal point for our lives.

What you heard from me, keep as the pattern of sound teaching, with faith and love in Christ.
—II Timothy 1:13

We must have faith in Christ which will produce submission to Him—first, in baptism as we become a new person, and, then, to bring forth the fruits of the spirit. Galatians 5:22 tells us what these are—love, joy, peace, patience, kindness, goodness, faithfulness, gentleness and self-control.

We will assemble with the saints on the first day of the week to worship, partake of the Lord's Supper, sing praises to God as we glorify His name, and hear His Will proclaimed. With personal endeavors and our financial means we will assist in spreading "the good news."

Another duty is recorded in Ephesians 6:2:

Children, obey your parents in the Lord, for this is right. Honor your father and mother—which is the first commandment with a promise, that it may go well with you and that you may enjoy long life on the earth.

One of the teachers of the law asked Jesus, "Of all the commandments, which is the most important?" "The most important one," answered Jesus, "is this: 'Love the Lord your God with all your heart and with all your soul and with all your mind and with all your strength.' The second is this: 'Love your neighbor as yourself.' There is no commandment greater than these."
—Matthew 22:35-36

How can we be sure that we are pleasing God in our religious life?

Religion that God our Father accepts as pure and faultless is this: to look after orphans and widows in their distress and to keep oneself from being polluted by the world.
—James 1:27

A very necessary ingredient that will produce soundness is an attitude of selflessness, compassion and service to others.

For even the Son of Man did not come to be served, but to serve, and to give his life as a ransom for many.

—Matthew 20:28

But do not use your freedom to indulge the sinful nature (flesh); rather, serve one another in love.

—Galatians 5:13

We must not be guilty of name calling and finger pointing, particularly, when we don't have the facts, just "hear say." This is not demonstrating love, kindness, or gentleness. Our enemy and adversary, Satan, is alert and cunning, ever scheming to trap us.

Satan himself masquerades as an angel of light.

—II Corinthians 11:14

Be self-controlled and alert. Your enemy the devil prowls around like a roaring lion looking for someone to devour. Resist him, standing firm in the faith.

—I Peter 5:8-9

Nothing pleases Satan more than to have God's people at odds with one another.

There is nothing confusing or complicated about the way we are to conduct our lives to be pleasing to God, and, thus, assuring soundness and wholeness. Our hearts may need transformation in order to be more loving, forgiving, compassionate, and spiritual; our worship may need to undergo some alterations so that our praise and glorification to God will be more meaningful, but if we will permit Christ to lead the way, then we will know that we have the truth and that the storm clouds will not be a threat.

Buy the truth and do not sell it; get wisdom, discipline and understanding.

—Proverbs 23:23

The people were amazed at his (Christ's) teaching, because he taught them as one who had authority, not as the teachers of the law.

—Luke 4:32

God's Unchanging Hand

Do you ever change your mind? I'm sure you do. They say it's a woman's prerogative to change her mind, but men change their minds too.

Change surrounds us; it is in everything. We welcome the change in the seasons. We enjoy the change from rain to sunshine; and sometimes in reverse, we are glad to see the rain after a drought.

We change jobs sometimes out of necessity, other times because of choice. We change location of our homes, from city to city, or from state to state.

Our habits change and our attitudes change. When someone says, "I'll never change my mind about thus and so," take note, as often times that person may have a change of heart and mind—sometimes not.

Some of the changes in today's world are tragic. The change in moral values—it seems anything goes. We have a terrible drug scene with crime and violence so rampant that all of us must be on guard constantly as we go about our daily lives. America and the whole world must change or we will go down like Sodom, Gomorrah, and Rome.

Then there are the changes in our physical bodies. The baby changes to a young child very quickly, then to adolescence, and on to adulthood, and at last to an old person. This is natural—the way God planned our lives to be.

Now the word "change" looms in the spiritual realm. Is there anything that needs changing? If so, what criterion do we use to determine the changes?

God changed worship from the Mosaic law to the freedom in worship under the law of Christ. When Christ died for our sins and was resurrected to a new life, the change took place in the way we are saved.

As we live in "the last days," do we need to change anything? More than likely, we do. Don't panic! I'll try to explain. When we accept Christ as our Savior and guide, and submit to the waters of baptism, our lives change, necessarily, for we take a new direction. I think all of us understand this. There will be changes in our words, thoughts, and actions; but after that, what about changes? From time to time we may slip back into the old lifestyle. Therefore, we have to be on guard constantly and make the necessary changes as we go.

If you have been God's child for a long time, you may have become complacent, set in your ways, dogmatic, or stubborn. Have you become a bench warmer? I hope not. Are you completely satisfied to sit back in ease and let things drift along? If so, it is time to take inventory. When you sing the old, old songs do they still have meaning for you? Or are the songs so familiar that you hardly notice the words anymore? All of us are guilty from time to time of allowing our minds to wander and it is so easy to become self-satisfied with the status quo.

I'm not advocating doing away with all the old songs, but we need to update our songs and our singing so that we can have more spirituality in our worship. Concentrate on the words; what do they really mean and how are they relevant in our lives? You may have noticed that from time to time throughout this book I have emphasized the need to improve our worship in song.

We know that God does not change, and we know that the gospel was delivered once and for all. The way we accept Christ and come into his saving grace will never change. The way we are to live as His children in all godliness will not change.

> *I will give you the keys of the kingdom of heaven; whatever you bind on earth will be bound in heaven, and whatever you loose on earth will be loosed in heaven.*

> —Matthew 16:19

At the time of Peter's confession that "You are the Christ," Christ instructed Peter and the other disciples to bind what heaven binds and loose what heaven has decreed.

> *I warn everyone who hears the words of the prophecy of this book: If anyone adds anything to them, God will add to him the plagues described in this book. And if anyone takes words away from this book of prophecy, God will take away from him his share in the tree of life and in the holy city, which are described in this book.*

> —Revelation 22:18-19

What areas, then, need investigation? From the above scriptures we have learned about binding and loosing, and in Revelation we have learned that we cannot add to or take from the things written in the Bible.

Opinions and traditions must be scrutinized to make sure we aren't binding things that must be loosed. At the same time, we must not loose anything that needs to remain bound.

I'm not going to tell you what any of these things are. Instead, I challenge you to take a fresh look into all matters in the spiritual realm. Read and study your Bible with diligence, not just as a daily devotional.

If your Bible is a bit dusty, now is the time to again travel through its pages and renew your spirit and your understanding of what God is saying to you. The Bible is exciting and refreshing each time you read it, and it holds the secret and the key to eternal life.

You are the one to make the decision as to whether you should discard an opinion which has been held because of self-will or simply because that's the way it has always been. Examine these areas to make sure the ones you are holding to so firmly are Bible principles, not just tradition or opinion.

All of us may need to attain a spiritual revival and then with new vitality and enthusiasm for the good news of the gospel, we can face the world confidently as we hold to God's unchanging hand.

Hold to God's Unchanging Hand
Time is filled with swift transition—Naught of earth unmoved can stand—
Build your hopes on things eternal, Hold to God's unchanging hand.

The Lamp That Lights Our Way

Were you afraid of the dark when you were young? Maybe you are still uneasy and apprehensive in total darkness because there is something ominous in situations without light.

In order to have light in darkness, there must be a light-giving vessel. Probably the first device to produce artificial light was a hollowed out stone in which plant fibers were used as a wick to burn fat as fuel.

Later, the Romans made ornate lamps of bronze or pottery which burned oil and could be placed on a table or suspended by a chain. During the Middle Ages an oil lamp called a cruse appeared in Scotland. This lamp was made of iron and had a trough for holding the oil, and the American colonists made cruses called Betty lamps which burned fish oil or whale oil.

Gas lamps came into use in the 1800's for homes as well as street lamps, but it was the invention of the electric lamp by Thomas Edison in 1879 that produced more and better light. This eventually brought about drastic changes in lighting to the extent that we are now almost totally dependent on electricity. When there is a power outage we are made painfully aware of how much we depend on electricity.

What about spiritual lamps, and what is the fuel necessary to make a light bright enough to lead us as we grope in the deep recesses of spiritual darkness?

Earlier, we learned that each one of us carries a basket, and now it is quite evident that we must carry a lamp. Did you say, "That's too much to carry?" Not true. Just as the lighthouse beams guides the ships to safety; just as signals keep trains on the right tracks; just as radar screens lead planes through the correct lanes; and just as headlights are necessary on cars, we must have a lamp to light our way.

You are my lamp, O Lord, the Lord turns my darkness into light.
—Psalm 18:28

The Lord is my light and my salvation; whom shall I fear?
—Psalm 27:1

...in thy light shall we see light.
—Psalm 36:9

Thy word is a lamp unto my feet, and a light unto my path.
—Psalm 119:105

These scriptures tell us that God is our lamp and that he turns our darkness to light. In addition, God's word is a lamp for our feet and a light for our path.

For the commandment is a lamp and the law is light....
—Proverbs 6:23

...when I sit in darkness, the Lord shall be a light unto me.
—Micah 7:8

We must have fuel for our lamps in order to have illumination; we must not be like the foolish virgins who failed to have oil in their lamps (Matthew 25:2).

In Isaiah 9:2 we read the prophecy of Christ's birth which refers to the coming Messiah as a great light: "The people that walked in darkness have seen a great light."

Our spiritual lamps have many facets as recorded by Matthew in describing Christians as lamps.

Ye are the light of the world.
—Matthew 5:14

Let your light so shine before men that they may see your works and glorify your Father which is in heaven.

—Matthew 5:16

Children enjoy the song, "This Little Light of Mine," and they are so enthusiastic and animated as they sing, "put it under a bushel—No!—this little light of mine, let it shine all the time."

When we hear, believe and become Christ's disciples, and when we confess His name as Lord, repent and submit to baptism, the lamp is placed in our hands to begin our pilgrimage as God's obedient children.

For ye were once darkness, but now are ye light in the Lord: walk as children of light.

—Ephesians 5:8

But if we walk in the light, as he is in the light, we have fellowship one with another, and the blood of Christ Jesus his Son cleanses us from all sin.

—I John 1:7

Do you know the song, "How Shall the Young Secure Their Hearts?"

How shall the young secure their hearts, and guard their lives from sin?
Thy word the choicest rules imparts to keep the conscience clean.
Tis, like the sun, a heav'nly light that guides us all the day;
And thro' the dangers of the night, a Lamp to lead our way.

Have you stopped to think what this song is saying? Much too often, I believe, we sing the words of a song without thinking about the true meaning. Read the words of this song again.

What is the lamp that leads the way and guards our lives from sin? If you say, "God's word," you are right. We know also that God is light and Christ is light.

God is light, and in him is no darkness at all.

—I John 1:5

When Jesus spoke again to the people, he said, "I am the light of the world. Whoever follows me will never walk in darkness, but will have the light of life."

—John 8:12

116

With the Word (Holy Spirit) dwelling in our hearts, and with the fuel of good deeds in our lamps, we know that our lamps are shining brightly, all for the glory of God.

For God, who said, "Let light shine out of darkness," made his light shine in our hearts to give us the light of the knowledge of the glory of God in the face of Christ.

—II Corinthians 4:6

In the last chapter of the Bible we read the beautiful description of heaven, and once again we see the importance of light.

The city does not need the sun or the moon to shine on it, for the glory of God gives it light, and the Lamb is its lamp.

—Revelation 21:23

Don't let the light in your lamp go out!

That ye may be blameless and harmless, the sons of God, without rebuke, in the midst of a crooked and perverse nation, among whom ye shine as lights in the world; Holding forth the word of life....

—Philippians 2:15, 16

Comrade of Compassion

From my earliest remembrance I enjoyed Bible stories. My very early days were in the 1920's, and no visual aids were used in the telling of the stories; there were no pictures, no graphics, and not even the now obsolete flannel boards. It was up to the teacher to depict the story in a way to make the events come alive to small children.

I was very fortunate since I had teachers who described things so vividly that I felt that I knew the characters personally. One of my teachers was my mother, and I, especially, enjoyed the way she presented these beautiful true stories.

I "saw" David, the shepherd boy, as he roamed the hills with his sheep. I pictured him with a lyre, and I could "hear" him playing and singing while seated under a fig tree as he took a rest from the heat of the sun at midday. I "sat" with the multitudes as they were fed with a little boy's lunch, and I applauded as the walls of Jericho came tumbling down. But the most impressive story of all was the parable of the Good Samaritan. I could "see" the man who had been robbed and beaten as he laid in the road, and I was so angry because the priest passed by on the other side, and then the Levite also passed by on the other side? How could they? Why would they refuse to help this poor man? Then the Samaritan came along.

> But a certain Samaritan, as he journeyed, came where he was; and when he saw him, he had compassion on him, and went to him, and bound up his wounds, pouring in oil and wine, and set him on his own beast, and brought him to an inn and took care of him.
> —Luke 10:33-34

It never occurred to me that I could have been the priest or the Levite. Of course, I would have been the Samaritan! But would I? I have always considered myself to be a caring, compassionate person, but when I reached more mature years I came face to face with the question, "Would I have been the Samaritan?" or would I have said, "I don't have the time and I don't want to get involved in the situation."

Am I a Samaritan today or do I pass by on the other side? It is a frightening question. What is the extent of our compassion? Is it limited to certain people; is it limited to certain areas, and under categorical circumstances also within boundaries?

As a rule, I believe that we are caring, sympathetic, and understanding with family members and friends, and we certainly want to extend compassion to God's family. Sometimes our compassion is only on the surface. Just saying, "I'm sorry," or "If I can do anything, let me know," is too general and does not get to the heart of the matter. Instead ask, "What can I do to help?" and better still, make suggestions of things that you would be willing to do.

Now, let's go a step further to people unknown to us. I know several women who for years have been volunteers at nursing homes and local hospitals. These ladies have gone regularly to these places where the atmosphere, at its very best, is not too pleasant, but they have done what they could in a quiet, unassuming manner, not looking for any kind of reward. I wish that I could say that I have been one of these women, but I can't.

Another good work is distributing Meals on Wheels—a depressing job but a satisfying one, I'm told. I'm not one of these either. If you think that my shortcomings are beginning to show, you are right.

There are many compassion ministries—prison, homeless shelters, refuge for battered women and children, and assistance to people who are far from home as they care for family members in hospitals.

An area that has my admiration is that of help to the people in the Third World countries. When I read and see on television the doctors and nurses feeding and treating the malnourished children, the elderly and infirmed, I have the utmost respect and esteem for these people. The pictures are so disturbing that I can hardly look, yet these humanitarians touch, feed, and treat these people in a loving, caring manner—this is indeed complete compassion.

What is our compassion level in regard to people who are suffering due to violation of natural laws and moral laws? If a person has almost literally smoked himself or herself to death, do we have the same degree of compassion that we would have for a person suffering from other types of illnesses?

What about the person who has abused alcohol to the extent that cirrhosis of the liver has developed? Are we as compassionate as we should be? Do you think that these diseases have been brought on by God as punishment? I hope you don't think so. These illnesses are the result of violation of natural laws that govern the order of the universe. If we play with matches, we get burned; if we run in front of a car, we'll be killed; if we jump from a cliff, we will have to suffer the consequences. God did not bring the disaster.

How do we react to the deadly social diseases so rampant in our world? We are repulsed by the devastation heaped upon the human body. Are we compassionate and should we be? Is God compassionate? And when Christ lived in the flesh, how did he react?

A man with leprosy came to him and begged him on his knees, "If you are willing, you can make me clean." Filled with compassion, Jesus reached out his hand and touched the man. "I am willing," he said. "Be clean!" Immediately the leprosy left him and he was cured.

—Mark 1:40, 41

Many times we look away from human suffering. We don't want to look into the eyes of starving children; we avoid the plight of the crippled and the maimed because we feel uncomfortable. We don't know what to say to people who are blind, and we sometimes neglect visits to the funeral home because it is sad and upsetting. This attitude does denote a certain sense of sorrow, but does it show real compassion?

I believe that you will agree that Jesus is our perfect example—He is our perfect guide and our perfect Savior. Therefore, we must look to Him for answers in the arena of compassion.

During the brief span of Christ's earthly existence he was the Great Healer. He was filled with compassion as he was confronted daily by many people with illnesses and deaths. His second miracle was the healing of the nobleman's son. He raised the dead, opened the eyes of the blind, unstopped the ears of the deaf, restored a withered hand, and healed the lepers. Jesus also had compassion on sinners as demonstrated in the account of the adulterous woman.

> *Jesus straightened up (after writing on the ground) and asked her, "Woman, where are they? Has no one condemned you?" "No one, sir," she said. "Then neither do I condemn you," Jesus declared, "Go now and leave your life of sin."*
>
> —John 8:10, 11

Just as Jesus did not condone sin but had compassion on the sinner, we must do the same. We are inclined to categorize sins. In our way of thinking some sins are more serious and repulsive than others. It is true that some sins produce different consequences and some sins affect lives to various degrees, but God has not divided sins into categories, neither has He indicated in any way that any one sin is worse than another.

> *Women exchanged natural relations for unnatural ones. In the same way men also abandoned natural relations with women and were inflamed with lust for one another.*
> *Men committed indecent acts with other men, and received in themselves the due penalty for their perversion.*
>
> —Romans 1:26-31

Following this passage is a list of sins: envy, murder, strife, deceit and malice. Also condemned were gossips, Godhaters, slanderers, insolent, arrogant and boastful, disobedient to parents, senseless, faithless, heartless, and ruthless.

> *But because of your stubbornness and your unrepentant heart, you are storing up wrath against yourself for the day of God's wrath, when his righteous judgment will be revealed.*
>
> —Romans 2:5

> *Do not be deceived: Neither the sexually immoral, nor idolaters, nor adulterers, nor male prostitutes, nor homosexual offenders, nor thieves, nor the*

greedy, nor drunkards, nor slanderers, nor swindlers will inherit the kingdom of God.

—I Corinthians 6:9-10

But among you there must not be even a hint of sexual immorality, or of any kind of impurity, or of greed, because these are improper of God's holy people. Nor should there be obscenity, foolish talk or coarse joking, which are out of place....No immoral, impure or greedy person—such a man is an idolater—has any inheritance in the kingdom of Christ and of God.

—Ephesians 5:3-6

If we really follow the example of Christ we will be a comrade of compassion, not merely sorrowful and sympathetic. We must not look in another direction, neither can we pass by on the other side. We cannot turn a deaf ear hoping that the unpleasant and tragic situation will go away.

It is imperative that we have compassion on every suffering human being, and we must not dwell on the reasons for the suffering. We cannot afford to have a "holier than thou" attitude. Each and every one of us is carrying a sack of sins; your sin may not be the same as mine, but, as we have seen from this study, God looks at each sin in the same light and to the same degree. All of us have our idols—not idols made of stone and bronze—but idols none the less. They may be greed, fame, power, or pleasure. The very best of us sin and fall short.

What is your attitude in the compassion department? Do you need to take a second look and rethink how you feel about this subject? I know that I need to be more aware and that I need to be more involved in showing compassion.

Let's resolve to do more in this area as we keep in the forefront of our lives the compassionate spirit of the Great Healer, our Lord and our Savior, Jesus the Christ.

Finally, all of you, live in harmony with one another; be sympathetic, love as brothers, be compassionate and humble.

—I Peter 3:8

Rewards of Righteousness

Rewards are offered for various reasons and under different circumstances. We offer children rewards for being good and making good grades; we reward them for doing chores and being especially helpful. Sometimes we even offer them rewards for sitting still and being quiet. Many years ago my husband told a younger brother, "If you will sit still for five minutes, I'll give you a quarter." It worked every time.

Rewards are offered for information that may be important in solving a crime, or help in finding a missing person. Athletes are given rewards for outstanding performances in sports, and I suppose we could consider scholarships for academic ability as rewards. The Nobel Awards are given for achievement in many different fields of endeavor. Even the dentist rewards us with a new toothbrush, and the doctor gives the child a lollipop.

What kind of rewards do we expect from God, and what does it actually mean to be righteous?

Before me every knee will bow; by me every tongue will swear. They will say of me, "In the Lord alone are righteousness and strength."
—Isaiah 45:23-24

But my salvation will last forever, my righteousness will never fail.
—Isaiah 51:6

Don't you think that the reward we are most desirous of is salvation and an imperishable inheritance in heaven? Earthly inheritances will be spent or lost through bad investments. At best, they are corruptible and perishable, but the inheritance we receive from Christ through our faith is unconditionally guaranteed by the resurrection of our Savior.

Praise be to the God and Father of our Lord Jesus Christ. In his great mercy he has given us new birth into a living hope through the resurrection of Jesus Christ from the dead, and into an inheritance that can never perish, spoil or fade....kept in heaven for you, who through faith are shielded by God's power until the coming of the salvation that is ready to be revealed at the last time.
—I Peter 1:3-5

We must remember that our reward for being righteous and our ultimate inheritance of eternal life is not for service rendered; our debt to God is so great that we can never pay enough. Our hope comes from Christ who paid the debt for us, and by His grace if we live righteous lives.

Righteousness is another way of saying holiness; to be righteous is to be godly, pure, and virtuous. What can we expect by living godly lives? Many things: peace and strength, and we will be in a proper relationship with God.

> *If only you had paid attention to my commands, your peace would have been like a river, your righteousness like the waves of the sea.*
> —Isaiah 48:18

> *Yet what is due me is in the Lord's hand, and my reward is with my God.*
> —Isaiah 49:4

God promised Abraham an heir and because of his faith in God he was rewarded with a son. We, too, will be rewarded through our faithfulness and steadfastness.

> *Do not be afraid, Abram, I am your shield, your very great reward.*
> —Genesis 15:1

We will be rewarded for obedience to God's laws.

> *The law of the Lord is perfect, reviving the soul....By them is your servant warned; in keeping them there is great reward.*
> —Psalm 19:7, 11

At times we may be tempted to take revenge for an injustice done to us, but we should never return evil for evil, but leave it in the hands of God to make things right.

> *The righteous will be glad when they are avenged...then men will say, "Surely the righteous still are rewarded; surely there is a God who judges the earth.*
> —Psalm 58:10-11

If it should become necessary for us to suffer persecution for the cause of Christ we can take comfort in the following passage:

> *Rejoice, and be exceeding glad: for great is your reward in heaven: for so persecuted they the prophets which were before you.*
> —Matthew 5:12

In this day and age, persecution would be, more than likely, in the form of ridicule for being godly and virtuous. We are bombarded on every hand by the world which has become engulfed in low morals, decaying principles, and all manner of corrupt ways of thinking and living. Sinful lifestyles are accepted now that only a few short years ago would have been unthinkable.

At one time a man's word was his bond—not anymore. It seems that integrity, ethics, and honesty have flown out the window. Unfortunately, our governments have succumbed to corrupt practices.

We, who call ourselves Christians, must do everything in our power to help restore the righteous lifestyle expected by God.

Righteousness exalts a nation, but sin is a reproach to any people.
—Proverbs 14:34

The place to start is in the home with our children and grandchildren, then in the schools and governments. It won't be easy, but we have to start somewhere even if it is on a small scale. Don't take a defeatist attitude thinking that one person can't do much.

Only when and if our world returns to godly living will our streets and homes be safe; only then will our families be intact, and only when governments return to the principles set forth by our founding fathers can we, once again, call ourselves a free nation under God. Only in righteousness is there life; in sin there is always death.

All human beings desire to be free—free from want, free from fear, free to choose and free to worship. The reward of righteousness will be the ultimate freedom—freedom in Christ. If we run the course with patience, if we keep our goal in sight, and if we rely on God for strength and courage, then the greatest reward of all will be ours—eternal life in the glory of our Savior, Jesus Christ.

For the Son of man shall come in the glory of his Father with his angels, and then he shall reward every man according to his works.
—Matthew 16:27

Behold, I am coming soon! My reward is with me, and I will give to everyone according to what he has done.
—Revelation 22:12

When the Last Page Is Turned

When you receive a new book are you tempted to turn to the last page and read it? Many people do this but I don't. I want the ending to be a surprise; also I might be disappointed and decide not to read the book at all.

There is a different book—the book of life. You can't read the last page at the beginning because you don't know which page will be the last, but you can make sure of the contents of your book of life and I'm sure that you would like for the last page to be full, not empty and void.

Chapter by chapter, page by page each one of us is writing the story of our sojourn on the earth. Maybe you haven't thought about it—maybe you should. Have you stopped lately to contemplate your mortality?

Some people live to be very old while some are taken from the earthly pathway in the middle years; still others are snatched away suddenly in their youth.

If you are young, are you living each day as if it were the last, not in fear and apprehension, but with faith and anticipation? You can bring joy and a refreshing breeze into the life of older people. You can do things for them that they no longer can do for themselves.

If you are an older person you have a mission also. Even though you are tired and weary, and overcome with burdens and infirmities, there is still a purpose for your life and service to God. A word, a smile, a note, or a phone call may be the thing most needed by someone. A hug to a small child, an arm around a friend, a hand clapped with another in understanding and love can brighten a day.

Who is this God that we serve? Do we completely understand?

He made the earth by his power; he founded the world by his wisdom and stretched out the heavens by his understanding.
—Jeremiah 51:15

He who forms the mountains, creates the wind, and treads the high places of the earth—the Lord God Almighty is his name.
—Amos 4:13

All of us need to stop and think—why are we here? Don't forget your purpose for being, and don't forget that you were created in the image of God and that you have an eternal spirit. You were put on this earth to glorify God as you serve Him and your fellow man.

Don't forget your goal! It is to live with God through endless ages, isn't it?

I have fought the good fight, I have finished the race, I have kept the faith. Now, there is in store for me the crown of righteousness, which the Lord, the righteous Judge, will award to me on that day—and not only to me, but also to all who have longed for his appearing.
—II Timothy 4:7, 8

May all who seek you rejoice and be glad in you; may those who love your salvation always say, "Let God be exalted."
—Psalm 70

Not one of us knows when the last page of our book of life will be turned; whether it will be today or years from now, we need to be on guard so that nothing will deter us from our mission.

Don't let a day go by without reading the Bible! Listen attentively as He talks to you. The Word is personal to each and everyone of us. Don't let a day go by without talking to God! Thank Him for your unlimited blessings; ask Him for help—help that only He can provide, and pray in behalf of others who need strength and encouragement.

Yet I am not ashamed, because I know whom I have believed, and am convinced that he is able to guard what I have entrusted to him for that day.

—II Timothy 1:12

Now listen, you who say, "Today or tomorrow we will go to this or that city, spend a year there, carry on business and make money." Why, you do not even know what will happen tomorrow. What is your life? You are a mist that appears for a little while and then vanishes.

—James 4:13, 14

As I have shared my thoughts, my convictions, my hopes and my faith with you in this book, I have been richly blessed. The study of God's word has taken on greater proportions as I have searched the Holy Scriptures for passages to fit the various themes.

I have a new, refreshing perspective, and I hope that you, too, have discovered anew the exciting truths revealed to us by the Holy Spirit through the pages of inspired scripture.

It is my prayer that each person who reads this book will find something of value and some new insight into the everlasting and eternal words of God—all to His honor and glory and praise forevermore. In the name of our precious Savior, Jesus Christ. Amen!

For we must all appear before the judgment seat of Christ, that each one may receive what is due him for the things done while in the body, whether good or bad.

—II Corinthians 5:10